KU-335-738

Contents

About this Book

This book is divided into five sections to cover the most important aspects of your visit to Portugal.

Viewing Portugal pages 5–14

An introduction to Portugal by the author
Portugal's Features
Essence of Portugal
The Shaping of Portugal
Peace and Quiet
Portugal's Famous

Top Ten pages 15–26

The author's choice of the Top Ten places to see in Portugal, each with practical information.

What to See pages 27–90

The four main areas of Portugal, each with its own brief introduction and an alphabetical listing of the main attractions
Practical information
Snippets of 'Did You Know…' information
4 suggested walks
4 suggested tours
2 features

Where To... pages 91–116

Detailed listings of the best places to eat, stay, shop, take the children and be entertained.

Practical Matters pages 117–24

A highly visual section containing essential travel information.

Maps

All map references are to the individual maps found in the What to See section of this guide.

For example, the town of Tavira has the reference ✚ 89E2 – indicating the page on which the map is located and the grid square in which the town is to be found. A list of the maps that have been used in this travel guide can be found in the index.

Prices

Where appropriate, an indication of the cost of an establishment is given by € signs: €€€ denotes higher prices, €€ denotes average prices, while € denotes lower charges.

Star Ratings

Most of the places described in this book have been given a separate rating:

✪✪✪ Do not miss
✪✪ Highly recommended
✪ Worth seeing

Viewing
Portugal

Above: *fishing boats, Tavira*
Right: *donkeys used to be
common in rural areas like
Sesimbra, but are increasingly
being replaced by more modern
transport*

Martin Symington's Portugal

Islands

Although beyond the scope of this book, the Portuguese state includes two self-governing archipelagos out in the Atlantic Ocean: warm, blooming Madeira and its more barren sister island Porto Santo off the coast of Morocco; and the volcanic mountain tops which are the Azores, poking out of the Atlantic, roughly two thirds of the way across, between Lisbon and New York.

Millions of holidaymakers have visited Portugal over the last thirty years. The great majority of them have been lured to the Algarve by the south coast's sandy coves, manicured golf links, gaily painted fishing boats and lively nightlife in the busy resorts; few are disappointed. Others explore the great cities of Porto and Lisbon, or seek out the swinging resorts of Estoril and Cascais on the Lisbon coast.

The real joy of travelling in Portugal is that it is still one of the least discovered corners of Western Europe. A feeling of isolation still permeates the character of this nation of 11 million souls out on the southwest extremity of the continent. Other than the Algarve, Lisbon area, Porto and a few other tourist spots, Portugal still neither gets, nor expects, many visitors. Consequently, there are boundless opportunities for travellers to get close to this beautiful country and its people.

In the lush, green Minho in the far north of the country, many a traveller has been overwhelmed by local hospitality – particularly people who have stayed in private homes under the *Turismo de Habitação* scheme (► 101).

Portugal offers true wilderness, too, in the remote Penêda-Gerêz and Montesinho national parks, and in the wilds of the Serra da Estrêla, the country's highest mountain range. Southwards, you need only drive a couple of hours from the Algarve's beach resorts to find the cork-forested plains of the Alentejo, sprinkled with dazzling white, Moorish-style villages.

These are the aspects of Portugal which travellers, fired with a spirit of adventure and a dose of curiosity, should try and explore.

Seaweed, a traditional fertiliser, is harvested on the Aveiro Ria, using long-prowed moliceiro *boats*

Portugal

by Martin Symington

Martin Symington is a prolific travel
journalist and author, contributing regularly
to British national newspapers and
numerous other publications in the UK and
overseas. He travels all climes from
the tropics to the arctic.
Other guide books he has written include
AA/Thomas Cook Travellers Denmark.
He was born and grew up in Portugal,
where he maintains close contacts and
continues to travel regularly. He lives in
Wiltshire with his wife and three children.

Above: *Pinhão station*

AA Publishing

Football scarves

Written by Martin Symington
Updated by Lindsay Bennett

First published 1998
Reprinted April 1999. Reprinted February 2000 (twice)
Reprinted 2001. Information verified and updated.
Reprinted June 2002; April 2003
Reprinted April 2004
**This edition 2005. Information verified and
updated.** Reprinted May 2005
Reprinted Jan and Apr 2006
Reprinted Feb and July 2007

Published by AA Publishing, a trading name of
Automobile Association Developments Limited, whose
registered office is Fanum House, Basing View,
Basingstoke, Hampshire RG21 4EA.
Registered number 1878835.

Find out more about
AA Publishing and the
wide range of travel
publications and services
the AA provides by
visiting our website at
www.theAA.com/travel

A03510

Colour separation: Keenes, Andover
Printed and bound in Italy by Printers Trento S.r.l.

Portugal's Features

Geography

Portugal lies at the southwest extremity of continental Europe, forming the western edge of the Iberian peninsula. The country's only neighbour is Spain, with whom the River Minho forms a natural border in the north. Eastwards a backbone of craggy mountains divides the old adversaries, while expansive plains stretch down to the sea.

Climate

The Algarve enjoys a Mediterranean-type climate with long hot summers, mild winters and more than 3,000 hours of sunshine a year, although there is always a possibility of rain between September and May.

In the Alentejo, the hinterland of the Beiras and the Alto Douro, summers can be searingly hot. Spring and autumn are cooler, with winters in the mountain regions getting very cold with sub-zero temperatures and snow in the Serra da Estrêla.

Porto and the Minho enjoy a temperate climate, with cooler temperatures year round, and the strong possibility of rain any time between autumn and spring.

Population

The current population is about 10 million, although around 3 million more Portuguese live as migrant workers in France, Germany, the USA, Canada, Venezuela and elsewhere.

Language

The national language is Portuguese. In written form, it appears similar to Spanish, but the sound is much more guttural, making it generally more difficult for foreigners to learn and understand.

Religion

About 99 per cent of the Portuguese population is Roman Catholic. There are small Protestant and Jewish communities.

General Figures

Portugal is roughly rectangular, 560km long from north to south, and 215km wide. Two great rivers, the Douro and the Tejo (Tagus) rise in Spain and flow across the country to their mouths at Porto and Lisbon respectively.

The highest peak in Portugal is Torre in the Serra da Estrêla at 1,993m. A metal post has been added to top the 2,000m mark.

Above: *port vineyards are hewn and blasted out of mountain sides in the wild Douro valley*

Essence of Portugal

Portugal is the last remaining relatively undiscovered country of Western Europe. Those with enough time on their hands to travel from one end to the other will discover a staggering variety of scenery, architecture and ways of life.

They will also find a country whose national character has been shaped by history, geography and centuries of warfare with Spain, Portugal's great Iberian rival. Portugal looks out to sea. Cut off from the rest of Europe, it has always had to do so. This explains why such a small nation became one of the great seafaring countries of the world.

Today, Portugal is a modern state and a member of the European Union, but the visitor need not dig very deep to find more ancient traditions.

Above: rustic clothes are gradually giving way to modern garb in rural areas
Below: donkey carts are still a feature of Algarve's backwaters

THE **10** ESSENTIALS

If you only have a short time to visit Portugal, or would like to get a really complete picture of the country, here are the essentials:

• **Walk along the quayside in Lisbon's Belém district**. Admire the great 'Manueline' showpieces of the Jerónimos Monastery and the Belém Tower. You will not fail to sense the spirit of the great Portuguese explorers (➤ 49–56).

• **Go to a *fado* house**. The songs you will hear lay Portugal's soul bare, and express the notion of *saudade* – a deep longing for something lost (➤ 114).

• **Stand on Europe's most southwesterly point**, Cabo de São Vicente. It is a suitably dramatic spot for the very corner of a continent. Ships on their way to or from the Mediterranean pass by incredibly close (➤ 18–19).

• **Visit Barcelos market** on a Thursday morning, and barter with the best of them (➤ 38).

• **Sit in the shade of an Alentejo cork tree** or go for a walk through a forest of these beautiful trees whose thick bark is prized all over the world.

• **Go to a village *festa***. These erupt all over the country, especially in summer, with religious processions, singing, dancing, eating and drinking as fireworks leave a whiff of gunpowder hanging in the air (➤ 116).

• **Walk round the walls of Silves castle**, and feel the wraiths of the Moors, for whom this was once the capital of *Al-Gharb* – 'the Western Land' (➤ 90).

• **Ride on a tram** – in either Lisbon or Porto. Choose one of the clanking, turn-of-the-century ones.

• **Eat a plate of sardines** grilled whole on charcoal. Have them plain, with just some lemon squeezed over them.

• **Drink a glass of port**. Then another. What more needs to be said? Only that you must try also try some chilled *vinho verde*.

Below: *Cabo de São Vicente, Europe's southwesterly extremity*

Below: *trams are a cheap and efficient way of getting around Lisbon*

The Shaping of Portugal

2000–1000 BC
Celtic invaders interbreed with the aboriginal tribes of Iberia, to produce the Celt-Iberian civilisation.

About 200 BC
Rome conquers Iberian peninsula, naming much of what is today's Portugal *Lusitania*.

About AD 100
Christianity introduced.

About AD 400
Waves of central European tribes invade the Iberian peninsula. Most are driven out by Visigoths, who are allied to the Romans.

711
North African Moors conquer the Iberian peninsula.

Prince Henry the Navigator initiated Portugal's age of exploration

About AD 800
Gradual Christian reconquest begins.

1139
Afonso Henriques wins battle of Campo Ourique against the Moors, and becomes first King of Portugal.

1249
Reconquest of the Algarve from the Moors is completed by King Afonso III.

1385
King João I routs the Castilians at the battle of Aljubarrota.

1386
King João marries Philippa of Lancaster and signs the Treaty of Windsor in alliance with England.

1415
Portugal's great era of discovery and colonial expansion begins with the capture of Ceuta in Morocco.

Left: *a statue of Vasco da Gama, another leading figure in the age of discoveries, in Évora*

1419–60
Under Prince Henry the Navigator, Portugal discovers Madeira and the Azores and explores the West African coast.

1496
Jews are forced to convert to Christianity or leave Portugal.

1498
Vasco da Gama discovers the sea route to India.

1500
Pedro Cabral is blown off course and accidentally discovers Brazil.

1578
King Sebastião launches lunatic invasion of Morocco. He and 15,000 men are slaughtered at Al Kasr Al-Kabir.

1580
Philip II of Spain takes advantage of Portugal's weakness and usurps throne.

1587–96
British attack Algarve ports as part of war against Spain.

1640
Following widespread anti-Spanish feeling, Duke of Braganza crowned King João IV, restoring Portugal's independence.

1755
Lisbon and much of southern Portugal, destroyed by earthquake.

1807
Napoleon invades Portugal for failing to support blockade of Britain.

1808–11
The Peninsular War. British forces under Wellington defeat the French and drive them out of Portugal.

1908
King Carlos and his heir assassinated in Lisbon.

1910
Younger son of Carlos, King Manuel II forced into exile. The Republic proclaimed.

1910–26
Country becomes ungovernable, undergoing 45 changes of government.

1916–18
Portugal fights with Allies in World War I.

1926
Army takes over.

1932
Army appoints António Salazar as prime minister. Effectively a dictator, he stays in office until 1968.

1939–45
Portugal remains neutral through World War II.

1960–74
Portugal fights guerilla wars in African colonies of Angola, Mozambique and Guinea-Bissau.

Sir John Moore retreats to Corunna during the 19th-century Peninsular War

1968
Salazar suffers a stroke and is replaced as prime minister by Marcelo Caetano.

1974
Right-wing regime overthrown by young left-wing army officers in almost bloodless coup.

1974–6
Series of coups and counter-coups culminating in the establishment of democracy. African colonies given independence and descend into civil wars.

1986
Portugal joins the European Community.

1998
Expo '98 World exposition held in Lisbon.

1999
Macau, Portugal's last colony, handed back to China.

2000
Portugal assumes presidency of the European Union.

2001
Lisbon is chosen as European City of Culture.

2003
Portugal's countryside is ravaged by fires destroying thousands of acres of forest and crops.

2004
Portugal plays host to the 2004 European football championships.

Peace & Quiet

Long swathes of dunes and cold, rough seas fringe the Minho coast

West Coast Beaches

To escape the crowds basking on the Algarve's golden sand throughout the summer, head for the west coast. The sea is cooler and rougher, and it can be windy, but there is a genuine sense of isolation. The sandy beaches of Bordeira, Castelejo and Arrifana are the size of athletics stadiums, backed by cliffs sheltering them from the wind. A few serious surfers are attracted here by the great, white Atlantic rollers which break out to sea and rush in noisily. Further north, around Odeceixe, the sand softens to a sandy estuary of wetlands, populated by dazzling white egrets.

Ria Formosa Natural Park

This is a protected area of wetlands, salt-marshes, lagoons and salt pans, around and extending east of Faro, the Algarve's capital. Public access is restricted for conservation reasons but there are several different points around the perimeter where birdwatchers can go to spot egrets, spoonbills and teal.

Berlenga Islands

Lying about 10km offshore and home to huge colonies of seabirds, these are the only islands off the coast of mainland Portugal. They can be visited on day trips from the port of Peniche, near Óbidos (➤ 23) between June and September. Shags, herring gulls and guillemots nest on the cliffs. It is possible to camp overnight or stay at the main island's very basic hostel (☎ 262 750331).

The Aveiro Ria

This great, brackish lagoon (commonly known as the Ria), joined to the sea by a narrow neck of water, spreads its finger-like inlets out across the flat, marshy land, extending 40km in total from Ovar in the north, down to Mira, south of the sea mouth. The rich bird life to be seen here includes herons, egrets, wildfowl and abundant snipe and other waders.

A hump-backed bridge over the Ria north of Aveiro takes the N327 on to the long, narrow spit of sand dunes, pine woods and marshes between the Ria and the sea, leading up to Ovar. There are several places to stop and swim.

Penêda-Gerês National Park

Bordering Spain in the far north of the country, these mountains include some of the wildest, most dramatic scenery Portugal has to offer. This is a gorse and boulder-strewn wilderness splintered by ravines and noisy streams, and fringed by granite peaks where buzzards and kestrels soar. There are waymarked walking trails and campsites within the park.

Montesinho Natural Park

Up in the far, northeast corner of the country, this is Portugal at its most remote. The park begins just north of Bragança, and extends up to the mountains which form a natural border with Spain. This giant hump of wild and exposed upland, dotted with huge, ancient and magnificent chestnut trees, is richer in wildlife than anywhere else in the country. You may see hares leaping through the heather, and birds of prey hovering overhead. The plentiful wild boar are nocturnal and seldom seen; so are the packs of wolves, which can sometimes be heard howling on a winter's night.

Wild Wolves

Packs of wolves roam isolated pockets of Portugal's remotest forests. They can sometimes be heard howling at night in the Serra da Estrela, or in the Montesinho Natural Park, where they cross from Spain in winter. Sightings are rare, but the image of a long-toothed, salivating beast is imprinted on the mind of every Portuguese child.
At Val Du Guarda near Malveira north of Cascais and Estoril, there is the Iberian Wolf Sanctuary (☎ 261 785037; open to visitors Sat–Sun 10–4), where a pack of wolves live in a natural environment.

The marshes and salt pans of the Aveiro Ria spread finger-like across the Beiras landscape

Portugal's Famous

Vasco da Gama

In the history of a nation which shaped the course of world history by the exploits of its explorers, the name of one such explorer stands head and shoulders above all others: Vasco da Gama.

Born in the ocean-side village of Sines on the Alentejo coast in about 1460 (the exact date of his birth remains uncertain), Vasco da Gama grew up looking out to sea with the scent of ozone in his nostrils.

As a young man, the stocky, black-bearded da Gama joined the King's household, trained as a sea pilot and took part in several expeditions along the West African coast, before being selected, in 1497, to lead the greatest quest of all – to discover for good and all, whether or not a sea route to India existed. If it did, untold riches would flow from the trade in spices between Europe and the East.

After a night spent awake and in prayer, Vasco da Gama set sail from Belém on 7 July 1497 with four ships and a crew of 170. He followed the route pioneered by Bartolomeu Dias down to the Cape of Good Hope. On 25 December he came ashore east of the cape, naming this land Natal ('Christmas' in Portuguese), as this province of South Africa is still called today.

Da Gama and his little fleet then became the first Europeans ever to sail up the East African coast. They dropped anchor at Malindi, in present day Kenya, and engaged the services of an Arab pilot, already skilled at navigating the Arabian Sea.

The final leg of the outward voyage took just 26 days. On 18 May 1498 Vasco da Gama reached Calicut on the Malabar coast of western India. The Portuguese were initially regarded with suspicion and their gifts from King Manuel of Portugal were scorned. However, three months later, they set sail for home with a cargo of spices.

The return to Portugal was more hazardous, with storms and scurvy taking heavy tolls. In September 1499, more than two years after he had left, Vasco da Gama sailed up the Tagus and docked at Belém amid scenes of great jubilation. Only two ships had survived the return journey, and of the 170 crew, only 55 came home.

Os Lusíadas

Portugal's greatest literary work, *Os Lusíadas* (The Luciads), by Luis de Camões, is an epic poem triumphantly celebrating Vasco da Gama's discovery of the sea route to India. The beautifully cadenced prose describes the journey, at times seen through the eyes of Greek gods and goddesses in homage to Western civilisation's Greek roots. *Os Lusíadas* is translated into many languages.

Above: *Vasco da Gama, discoverer of the sea route to India*

Top Ten

Above: *Mosteiro dos Jerónimos*
Right: *jewellery, Museu Calouste Gulbenkian*

1
Alcobaça

58B3

20km south of Batalha

Apr–Sep daily 9–7;
Oct–Mar 9–5

Buses from Lisbon (2
hours) and Leiria (45
mins)

Tourist Office: Praça 25
de Abril, opposite abbey
(☎ 262 582377)

Few

Apr–Sep, moderate;
Oct–Mar, cheap

*Famous lovers Pedro and
Inês are entombed toe to
toe, so that the first thing
they see in resurrection
will be each other*

*One of the most beautiful and atmospheric
buildings in Portugal and a shrine to a
poignant love story.*

The Real Abadia de Santa Maria de Alcobaça (the Royal
Abbey of St Mary) was built on the orders of King Afonso I
to fulfil a promise he had made to God before a victory
over the Moors at Santarem. It was given to the Cistercian
order and became immensely rich and powerful, in the
finest traditions of medieval monasticism. The monks
remained at Alcobaça until the Abbey's confiscation during
repression of religious orders in the 19th century. Today,
the monastery still dominates this small agricultural town
surrounded by fruit-growing estates and vineyards.

The church, the largest in Portugal, is gloriously
spacious and built in a refreshingly simple style, as are
the 14th-century cloisters where a calming aura lingers,
especially if you are able to wander round in silence.
More worldly are the gigantic kitchens and monastic
cooking utensils.

But it is the tombs of Dom Pedro and Inês de Castro
which attract the greatest attention. The pair are
Portuguese history's irrepressible lovers – Pedro was a
prince and Inês the daughter of a nobleman from Galicia
with whom he had fallen in love. His father, King Afonso,
had her murdered to avoid allowing the Galicians influence
in Portuguese affairs. Pedro rebelled against his father and
two years later became king, holding the memory of Inês
dear for the rest of his life. Both were buried at Alcobaça in
tombs with intricate carvings telling their story; the tombs
are toe-to-toe so that the first thing they see on
Judgement Day will be each other.

2
Batalha

Batalha is one of the architectural jewels of Portugal and a symbol of independence from Spain.

Batalha means 'battle', referring to a promise by King João I that if he defeated the Castilian army, he would build a great monastery and dedicate it to the Virgin. The victory duly took place in 1385 at nearby Aljubarrota; although greatly outnumbered, João's military commander, Constable Nun' Alvares Pereira, put the Castilians to flight. The massive building project began in 1388, eventually becoming a Dominican abbey.

The towering honey-coloured church with its spires, pinnacles, flying buttresses and gargoyles comes startlingly into view as you round a corner on the N1. The sheer dimensions are awesome – the nave is 80m long by

➕ 36A1

✉ 11km south of Leiria

🕐 Apr–Sep daily 9–6; Oct–Mar 9–5

🚌 Bus stop on Largo de Misericórdia

ℹ Tourist Office: Plaça Mouzinho de Alduquerque (☎ 244 765180)

♿ Few

✋ Apr–Sep, moderate; Oct–Mar, cheap

32m high. King João and his Queen, Philippa of Lancaster, lie entombed in the octagonal Capela do Fundador (Founders' Chapel), their stone-carved effigies resting, hand in hand, under a stone canopy emblazoned with the coats of arms of Lancaster and the House of Avis. Nearby lie the tombs of their six sons, including Prince Henry the Navigator.

Among the other finest features are the Capelas Imperfeitas (unfinished chapels), exuberantly decorated with carvings of Manueline flamboyance; the Royal Cloisters, with intricately carved Manueline embellishments to the original Gothic; and the beautifully vaulted Chapterhouse, containing the tombs of unknown soldiers killed in World War I and in the African wars.

Towering Batalha abbey, seen from the N1 road, is an awesome sight

3
Cabo de São Vicente
(Cape St Vincent)

*A raw, wild, windswept headland
at the very corner of Europe, punctuated with
a huge lighthouse.*

28A1

6km west of Sagres

Access to the cape at any time. No official timetable for the opening of the lighthouse

Buses from Sagres

None

Free

Cabo de São Vincente, 6km along the cliff top road from Sagres, is the most southwesterly promontory of Europe. Here the rock face is sheer and grey, dropping several hundred metres into the sea. Ships, on their way to the Mediterranean, pass by unbelievably close. Further out, sharks are caught from small fishing boats. Land-based anglers perch precariously on the cliff-edges, casting their long lines way down into the deep Atlantic. Tales are told of the less wary, hooking a sizeable fish and being yanked to their deaths, over the cliff.

Above: *the lighthouse at Cabo de São Vicente throws its beam 90km out to sea*

The only building is a lighthouse, which you can climb if it happens to be open – there are no published times – to see the 3,000-watt bulb which projects its beam 90km out to sea. Outside, stalls sell thick woollen shirts and socks; tourists, who often arrive wearing just shorts and T-shirts, make easy prey as they are caught unawares by the chill wind which blows even in summer.

For some, the cape appears a god-forsaken place – out on a bare, windswept plain dotted with scrub and the occasional stunted, crouching fig tree. The few nearby Moorish-style villages of whitewashed walls and red tiles are tightly huddled, as if sheltering from the wind. Others appreciate the raw, solitary beauty of this landscape.

In March, April, September and October, huge flocks of migrating birds use the cape as a staging post, on their journeys between Europe and Africa.

Opposite: *sharks are caught in the deep waters off Cabo de São Vicente*

4
Monsaraz

➕ 28B2

✉ Southeast of Évora, 7km off the N256

🍴 Restaurants and cafés, including Solar de Monsaraz (€€)

🚌 Daily bus service from Évora (45 mins)

ℹ Tourist Office: Largo Nuno Álvares (☎ 266 557136)

♿ Few

One of Portugal's most spectacular fortified hilltop villages, nestling within impregnable stone walls.

Monsaraz is one of a long chain of fortified villages near Portugal's eastern border with Spain, built for their commanding positions; Romans, Visigoths and Moors all had settlements here, before the Christian re-conquest. The village itself has a sleepy, medieval mien – the main street is too narrow for a car; park outside the main gate.

The present castle and formidable ramparts are 14th-century, built by King Dinis. In front of the pentagonal castle keep is a square where bullfights are held on feast days with villagers cheering from the walls.

The view from the parapet is stunning: the plains of the Alentejo stretch out endlessly towards the coast, whose outline just becomes visible on the horizon when the air is exceptionally clear. The rocky, meandering Guadiana river, to the east, provides a dramatic contrast, while Spain extends beyond like a crumpled rug.

Monsaraz is one of the most quintessential of Portuguese villages

There are several points of interest on Rua Direita, the cobbled main street, which is lined with houses embla-zoned with the coats of arms of wealthy 16th–17th-century families. The Paços do Concelho Tribunal building has a 15th-century fresco depicting a judge being tempted by an impish, bride-offering devil while simultaneously being drawn into the outstretched arms and majestic justice of Christ.

The Igreja Matriz parish church is also worth a look.

5

Mosteiro dos Jerónimos
(Jerónimos Monastery)

*The crowning glory of Manueline architecture,
built on riches which followed the discovery
of trade routes to the east.*

Jerónimos is the classic example of Manueline architecture, the home-grown style through which a tiny nation proclaimed its greatness to the world. The monastery is built on the site of the Santa Maria hermitage, which Prince Henry the Navigator founded in 1460, the year of his death. This was hugely embellished by Dom Manuel in the following century to commemorate Vasco da Gama's discovery of the sea route to India in 1498.

Accordingly, the buildings are adorned with ocean-going and oriental motifs such as seahorses, elephants, ropes and armillary spheres, all elaborately carved in stone. The southern façade, looking out over the Tagus estuary, is sensationally grand. A bearded statue of Prince Henry stands at the south portal. Dom Manuel and his wife Dona Maria preside over the west portal, in the company of the four evangelists.

Most breathtaking of all is the cavernous interior; six great supporting columns are styled as colossal palm trees with fanned ribbed vaulting as their fronds. Inside are the tombs and stone effigies of several kings supported by elephants, and of two of Portugal's greatest heroes – Vasco da Gama himself, and Luis de Camões, who told the story of his discoveries in the epic poem *Os Lusíadas* (► 14).

The monastery was seriously damaged in the 1755 earthquake but many splendid features survived unscathed, including the elaborate and majestic west portal. The cloisters are on two storeys, carved with fantastic and surreal animals and distorted human figures secreted among intricate vegetation.

Right: *Manueline buildings – the status symbols of a superpower*

✝	Off map 52A1
✉	Belém, Lisbon
🕐	Tue–Sun 9–6:30
🚌	Buses from the Baixa district; tram 15
🚉	On the Avenida de Brasília
⛴	Ferry to Trafaria, across the Tagus
♿	Few
✋	Church free; Cloisters moderate

21

6
Museu Calouste Gulbenkian

*An astounding collection of artistic riches
from across the centuries,
bequeathed by the oil magnate.*

🔲 Off map 52C4

✉ Avenida da Berna 45,
Lisbon

🕐 Tue–Sun 10–6. Modern
Art Museum Tue–Sun
10–5:45. Closed public
holidays

🍴 Café-bar (€€)

🚇 Metro S Sebastião
Palhavã

🚌 Bus 16, 26, 31, 46, 56

♿ Good

🎫 Tue–Sat cheap,
Sun free

*A 14th-century mosque
lamp is one of thousands
of treasures in the
Gulbenkian collection*

Calouste Gulbenkian was an Armenian oil magnate who, shortly after the turn of the century, acquired a five per cent share in the oil fields of Iraq. As the 20th century progressed, man's dependence on the internal combustion engine burgeoned and Gulbenkian grew phenomenally wealthy. In 1942 he adopted Portugal, neutral during World War II, as his homeland.

He died in Lisbon in 1955, bequeathing his vast array of treasures and huge fortune to the establishment of a foundation for 'charitable, artistic, educational and scientific' purposes. The foundation's assets now make it the largest charity in Europe.

The museum, set in beautiful green gardens, was opened by the foundation in 1969, and includes seven principal collections: Egyptian art; Graeco-Roman art; Middle Eastern and Islamic art; Oriental art; a collection of French ivories; painting and sculpture (including works by Rembrandt, Rubens, Gainsborough and Manet, and a superb marble statue of Diana by Houbon) and furniture and furnishings.

The museum also houses smaller, rare collections, such as snuff boxes, French bookbindings, European ceramics, art nouveau jewellery and gold and silver work.

Across the gardens from the main museum is the Centro de Arte Moderna (Modern Art Centre), a new extension opened in 1983. The centre houses both permanent and temporary exhibitions, with a strong emphasis on 20th-century Portuguese artists such as Almada Negreiros, who was the founder of the school of Portuguese Modernism. There is also some excellent modern sculpture on display in the centre, including work by Henry Moore.

7
Óbidos

An enchanting hilltop town, beloved of artists and poets and traditionally given as a wedding gift by Portuguese kings to their queens.

Óbidos is enclosed within massive, crenellated 13th-century walls punctuated with huge, round towers out of all proportion to the Lilliputian buildings within. Not a single modern structure is to be found; instead, there are scaled-down versions of typically Portuguese baroque churches, cottages, worn stone staircases and alleyways.

There are about 5,000 inhabitants, including many poets and artists drawn by the romanticism of Óbidos, and villagers whose families have lived here for generations, and who still have their diminutive vegetable patches at the base of the great walls.

✚ 58B3

✉ 22km inland from Peniche

🚌 Bus stop by the Porta da Vila

🚉 Train station outside the walls. Lisbon 2 hours

ℹ Tourist Office: Rua Direita, in car park at entrance to town (☎ 262 959231)

♿ Very difficult – many steps and steep sections

At the highest point, set against the walls, is the castle, which became a royal palace in the 16th century. It has been converted into an atmospheric *pousada*.

A leisurely walk around the entire walls, which includes some fairly steep climbing, takes about an hour. A good place to start is at the main gate at the bottom of the town, but there are several other staircases up the 14m-high ramparts to tremendous vantage-points from which to watch the town's goings-on. Looking beyond the walls, there are wonderful vistas over the Laguna de Óbidos (Óbidos Lagoon) – the inlet is now silted up but it once made Óbidos a sea port.

To look out west from the walls, towards the coast and horizon beyond as a blood-red sunset dims into twilight, can be an achingly romantic experience.

Artists and poets love the romantic town of Óbidos

23

8
Serra da Estrêla

🕂 37C2

🍴 Restaurants of all categories in the region

🚌 All the main towns of the area are connected by bus, though services are often scant

🚉 Covilhã has a train station, 4km out of town

ℹ️ Tourist Offices: Serra da Estrala regional office, Avenida Frei Heitor Pinto (☎ 275 319560)

This range of soaring mountains, interspersed with glacial valleys, is a real treat for hikers and nature-lovers.

Between Coimbra and the Spanish border is Portugal's highest mountain range and national park – the rugged Serra da Estrêla, whose crowning peak, the Torre, reaches almost 2,000m. Yet despite having some of the most spectacular scenery in the country, this sparsely populated region is still relatively unknown to outsiders.

When snow falls, a few optimistic skiers make for the two very limited runs which constitute the sum total of Portuguese wintersports; in spring the occasional lonesome nature-lover can be found on the wild, flower-blanketed mountainsides; in autumn you might come across a huntsman dangling a hare or partridge from his belt; in summer the streams dry up and the verdant valleys turn brown and inhospitable.

Nevertheless, a diversion through the Serra da Estrêla is highly recommended for those driving between Lisbon or the Alentejo and the north with time to spare. Particularly sensational are the N232 between Manteigas and

Above: *In winter snow falls on the Serra da Estrêla, Portugal's highest mountain range*

Opposite: *Tavira grew rich on tuna, and is still a fishing community*

Gouveia, and the Vale Glaciario do Zêzere (Zêzere Glacial Valley) which connects the N232 just south of Manteigas, with the N239 to Covilhã. The latter junction is a short distance from the Torre. There is a wonderfully located modern *pousada* (➤ 103) near Manteigas which is an excellent base for touring or walking.

Look out for the rich, creamy Serra da Estrêla cheese made from ewes' milk and sold by the roadside in pats wrapped in paper. The runny version is the tastiest, oozing out of cracks in its rind.

9

Tavira

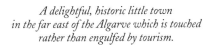

*A delightful, historic little town
in the far east of the Algarve which is touched
rather than engulfed by tourism.*

One of the Algarve's most beautiful towns lies beyond the marshes, salt pans, lagoons and flat sandy islands east of Faro. A string of elegant, 18th-century classical façades lines the waterfront along the River Gilão, spanned by two bridges, one of them originally Roman though most of the existing structure is 17th century. There are also gardens fronting the river, adjacent to the arcaded central Praça da República, and a covered market.

Tavira's prosperity was built on tuna fishing, mainly during the 16th to 18th centuries. Vast shoals used to migrate past this shoreline every summer, falling prey to the harpoons of the Tavira fleet. The giant, thrashing fish were hauled in and put to death by the fishermen amid bloody rituals which became known as the 'bullfights of the sea'.

This wealth accounts for the town's 21 churches; finest is Igreja do Carmo, where, beyond a simple façade, you are greeted by an unexpected riot of baroque. None of the churches has official opening times – just try your luck. There is also a ruined castle reached by a cobbled alley from the Praça da República. From here, there are some commanding views over the town.

Offshore is the Ilha de Tavira (Tavira Island), an 11km-long bar of sand which, despite the lack of shade, is one of the Algarve's best beaches east of Faro. Regular ferries leave from a jetty at Quatro Aguas, 2km from the town centre, and take just a few minutes.

89E2

30km east of Faro

Many restaurants
(€–€€€)

Bus station on the Rua dos Pelames, near the Praça da República

Train station at the end of Rua da Liberdade, 1km from town centre

Tourist Office: Rua da Galeria 9 (281 322511)

Few

10
Vila Nova de Gaia

30B1

Similar tours and tastings are conducted at the various lodges. Opening times are generally Mon–Fri 9:30/10–12 and 2:15–5:30. In summer, many also open on Sat

Restaurants of all categories in Gaia

Bus 33 from São Bento Station

Tourist Office: Avenida Diogo Leite 242 (☎ 22 379 0994)

The famous port lodges line the quayside at Vila Nova de Gaia

Discover the long and rich history of Portugal's most famous 'liquid asset', then sample the product.

Across the double-decker Dom Luis I bridge, opposite Porto, is Vila Nova de Gaia, home of port wine. Whitewashed onto red-tiled roofs, lit up at night in giant neon signs, and adorning the sails of traditional *barco rabelo* boats on the waterfront, are the familiar names of the great British port-shipping houses – Taylor, Graham, Cockburn, Sandeman – along with Portuguese houses such as Cálem and Ferreira.

Many of the port houses offer free guided tours of the so-called 'lodges' – a corruption of the Portuguese word *loja*, meaning 'warehouse'. You can wander through the ancient, cobwebbed corridors walled with barrels of port ageing in oak and learn how, in the 17th and 18th centuries, hostilities with France led British merchants to venture into the harsh, mountainous terrain of the upper Douro valley, in search of alternative sources of wine.

The brandy they added to preserve the wine during the hot journey downriver to Vila Nova de Gaia led to the birth of the fortifying process. Let your taste buds explore the many different styles of port: the aperitif, dry white port; light, amber-coloured tawny, made from wines up to a century old blended with fresh young wine; rich, full-bodied ruby port; and finally, vintage port, declared only in exceptionally good years, bottled after two years, matured in black bottles, and the flagship of every shipper's range.

Take care not to stagger into the Douro when the tour has finished and you re-cross the river to Porto.

What To See

Above: *attractive tiled window surrounds in Oporto*
Right: *azulejo tiles*

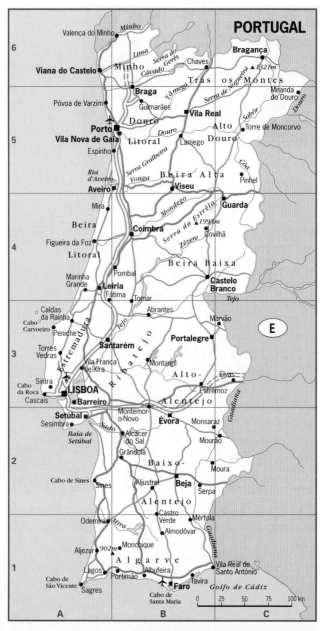

The North

The north is the cradle of the nation, where the Kingdom of Portugal was proclaimed in the 12th century. The centre of power shifted south many centuries ago, though the North remains richly historic. Towns such as Guimarães and Coimbra have both, for short periods, been the national capital.

Scenically the region is extremely diverse, from the lush and fertile Minho, north of Porto, described as the Costa Verde (Green Coast), to the austere mountains of the Serra da Estrêla and the grape-growing Douro valley. In between are the somnolent marches and salt pans of the Aveiro lagoon.

The quintessential Portuguese conservatism is more evident in the north – even in Porto, the country's second city – than in the south. For this reason, the people of the north are sometimes accused by their compatriots of backwardness.

*'Be sometimes to your
country true,
Have once the public good
in view.
Bravely despise Champagne
at Court,
And choose to dine at home
with Port.'*

JONATHAN SWIFT (1726)

Porto (Oporto)

Portugal's second largest city has a history going back some 4,000 years, making it one of the oldest towns in Europe. As a booming industrial centre some find it ugly. Others are quick to discover the charms of the old town and the vinous treats of Vila Nova de Gaia's port lodges (▶ 26).

For most visitors Porto's heart is in its old town, on the north bank of the river. The area is coloured by dense clusters of tall, dilapidated, red-tiled houses thrown haphazardly together in what looks like an oversized village spilling down from the city centre to the Ribeira district on the River Douro quay side.

Alleys and walkways, some of them tortuously steep, wind through this labyrinth of homes and artisans' workshops; women in voluminous skirts sell fruit,

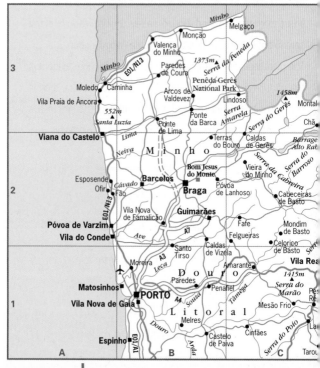

vegetables and sardines, while washing lines overhead flap with white sheets and brightly coloured clothing. Far from being a sanitised old town, as is found in so many European cities, this is a real living quarter, buzzing with activity.

Porto's ancient, rickety trams are a fun way to get around. Hop on one anywhere along the Douro quayside, and it will take you along the river to its mouth. However, most sightseeing can be done within a fairly short walk of the city centre, though you do need stamina for the steep gradients.

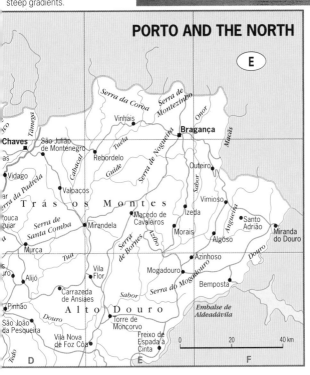

PORTO AND THE NORTH

E

What to See in Porto

FUNDAÇÃO DE SERRALVES
(SERRALVES FOUNDATION)   ✪✪✪

This new museum of modern art is housed in a striking post-modernist building in the grounds of the 1930s art deco Casa de Serralves. There are some outstanding contributions by contemporary Portuguese artists, as well as works by Picasso and Warhol.

IGREJA DE SÃO FRANCISCO CHURCH
(CHURCH OF ST FRANCIS)   ✪✪

One of the most amazing churches in Portugal, and to most tastes infinitely more beautiful than the Sé. Dazzling and intricate gilt work extends from ceiling to floor; it is said that there are over 400kg of pure gold inside.

MUSEU DE SOARES DOS REIS   ✪

Porto's principal museum occupies an 18th-century neo-classical home of the powerful Morães e Castro family, which later served as the headquarters of the Napoleonic forces during the Peninsular War. It is said that Wellington and his officers, having defeated the French and ousted Marshall Soult in 1809, ate their dinner here. The spectacle was probably rather more arresting than this somewhat

✚	Off map 33A3 west
✉	Rua D João da Castro 210
☎	22 615 6571
⏰	Tue–Sun 10–7
♿	Good
🖐	Moderate

✚	33B1
✉	Rua Infante D Henrique
⏰	Mar–Oct daily 9–6; Nov–Feb 9–5
♿	None
🖐	Moderate

✚	33A2
✉	Rua de Dom Manuel II
☎	22 339 3770
⏰	Wed–Sun 10–6, Tue 2–6. Closed public holidays
♿	Few
🖐	Moderate. Free Sun

down-at-heel museum, which displays 19th-and early 20th-century Portuguese art.

PALÁCIO DA BOLSA 🟢🟢🟢

The fine 19th-century granite and marble palace once housed the city's parliament and judiciary as well as the stock exchange. The guided tour of the palace takes you from echoing hall to sumptuous salon. It includes exhibits illustrating the history of Porto, and makes an excellent introduction to the city. The star attraction is the amazing Arab Room, decorated in brilliant Moorish style with gilding, stained-glass windows, painted stucco and a pastiche of the Alhambra in Granada, Spain.

➕ 33B1
✉ Rue Ferreira Borges
☎ 22 339 9000
🕐 Apr–Oct daily 9–7; Nov–Mar 9–1
🍴 Many restaurants and cafés in the nearby Ribeira
♿ Few
🎫 Moderate

Left: *the double-decker Dom Luis I bridge spans the Douro between Porto and Vila Nova de Gaia*

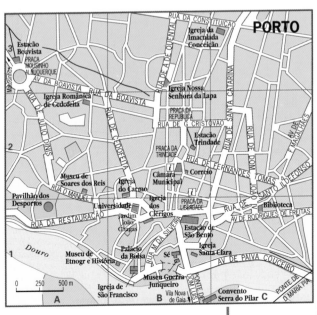

The Cathedral's high altar, typical of the ornate baroque which can be found in churches throughout Portugal

SÉ (CATHEDRAL) ✪✪

Porto's austere, grey cathedral, where King João I and Philippa of Lancaster were married in 1387, dates from the 12th century, when it was a fortress as well as a place of worship. This explains the presence of formidable granite battlements round the cloisters and forbidding square towers flanking the façade. However, the interior was completely re-vamped in baroque style during the 17th and 18th centuries. The two traditions sit rather inharmoniously together, and it is hard to describe the overall effect as either beautiful or inspiring. Don't miss the beautiful Romanesque rose window in the main western façade, or the lovely *azulejos* round the cloisters.

TORRE DOS CLÉRIGOS ✪

This soaring, rocket-like 75m-high granite tower of the Igreja dos Clérigos, has been a main feature of the Porto skyline since the building was completed in 1749. The exhausting climb to the top is up a spiral staircase of 225 worn steps, and is rewarded by fabulous views over the city, or severe vertigo, or both.

VILA NOVA DE GAIA (➤ 26, TOP TEN)

✚ 33B1
✉ Terreiro da Sé
🕐 Church daily 8:45–12:30, 2:30–6. Cloisters Apr–Oct Mon–Sat 8:45–12:30, 2:30–7, Sun 2:30–6; Nov–Mar Mon–Sat 9–12:15, 4:30–5:15, Sun 2:30–5:15
🍴 Many nearby cafés
♿ Few
💷 Church free; cloisters cheap
❓ Occasional classical concerts

✚ 33B1
✉ Rua S Filipe de Nery
☎ 22 200 1729
🕐 Church Mon–Sat 9–12, 3:30–7:30, Sun 10–1, 8:30–10:30. Tower Aug daily 10–7; Sep–Jul 9:30–1, 2–7
♿ None 💷 Cheap

Porto Walk

Starting at Estaçao de São Bento

Porto's central railway station is built on the foundations of Ave Maria convent, of which a few vestiges remain. Whether you are travelling by train or not, the station is worth visiting to see its fabulous collection of giant *azulejo* murals, depicting great events in the city's history.

Walk up the Avenida de Afonso Henriques to the Sé (Cathedral ➤ 34).

The main doors of the Sé give on to a pedestrianised square from where a stone staircase leads down into the warren of alleys which is Porto's old town. Twist down through this labyrinth, to emerge on Rua Infante Dom Henrique.

Turn right along Rua Infante Dom Henrique, till you reach the Praça do Infante Dom Henriques.

Visit the Palácio da Bolsa (➤ 33) and the adjacent Igreja São Francisco (➤ 32)

Walk back along Rua Infante Dom Henrique to the Feitoria Inglesa.

This fine 18th-century town house is a 'factory' in the old-fashioned sense of a meeting place of 'factors' or merchants rather than a manufactory. It is now the headquarters of the British Association of Port Shippers, and the interior can only be visited by invitation from a member.

Turn right and follow the Rua de São João down to the Praça da Ribeira square, leading on to the Cais da Ribeira.

The Cais da Ribeira are at the heart of the tourist area with restaurants, cafés, handicraft shops and an open air market. The vista across the river to Vila Nova da Gaia, with the double-decker Dom Luis I bridge looming large a little way upstream, is spectacular.

Follow the quay up to the bridge, continuing for a few metres along Avenida Gustave Eiffel, then climb the long stone staircase up to the Avenida de Vimara Peres, emerging by the Dom Luis Bridge at its upper level.

Distance
3km

Time
2–5 hours, depending on length of visits

Start point
São Bento Station
➕ 33B1

End point
Upper level, Dom Luis Bridge
➕ 33B1

Lunch
Taverna do Bebóbos (€€)
✉ Cais da Ribeira 24
☎ 22 313565

The Ribeira district is both a focus for tourism and a real living quarter

35

What to See in the North

AMARANTE ●●

Amarante is an enchanting little town which sits beside the Tâmega river, spanned by the photogenic 18th-century São Gonzalo bridge of honey-coloured granite. Terraces and verandahs overlook the willow-lined water where anglers cast for trout. A tiled cupola rises above the mellow stone of the 16th-century São Gonçalo convent. Inside is the tomb of São Gonçalo himself; votive offerings are left in the Chapel of Miracles.

Next to the church, part of the convent has been converted into a museum of modern art (**Museu Municipal Amadeo de Souza-Cardoso**) devoted to the works of local artists, with many works by Souzo-Cardoso himself.

+ 30C1
⊠ 56km east of Porto
? Colourful festival on first weekend Jun

São Gonçalo Church
⊕ Cloisters: Tue–Sun 10–12, 2–5
⅋ Few
✋ Free

Museu Municipal
⊠ Alameda Teixeira da Pascoaes
☎ 225 420 233
⊕ Daily 10–12:30, 2–5:30
⅋ Few
✋ Cheap

Votive offerings are left at the tomb of São Gonzalo

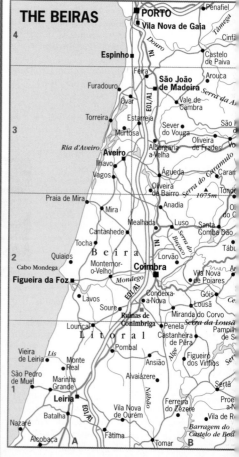

THE BEIRAS

PORTO
Penafiel
Vila Nova de Gaia
Cinfã
Douro
Tâmega
Castelo de Paiva
Espinho
Feira
Arouca
São João de Madeira
Furadouro
Serra da Ar
Ovar
Vale de Cambra
Torreira
Estarreja
Sever do Vouga
São
Murtosa
Oliveira de Frades
Vo
Ria d'Aveiro
Aveiro
Albergaria-a-Velha
Ílhavo
Caram
Vagos
Águeda
Serra do Caramulo
1075m
Praia de Mira
Oliveira de Bairro
Tonde
Mira
Anadia
Ol do C
Mealhada
Luso
Santa
Cantanhede
Serra do Buçaco
Comba Dão
Tocha
Beira
Lorvão
Tábu
Quiaios
Montemor-o-Velho
Coimbra
Cabo Mondega
Mondego
Vila Nova de Poiares
Ar
Figueira da Foz
Condeixa-a-Nova
Góis
Ce
Lávos
Soure
Lousã
Miranda do Corvo
Ruínas de Conímbriga
Serra da Lousã
Lourical
Penela
Pampilh de S
Litoral
Castanheira de Pêra
Vieira de Leiria
Lis
Monte Real
Pombal
Alge
Figueiró dos Vinhos
Ser
São Pedro de Muel
Marinha Grande
Ansião
Alvaiázere
Sertã
Leiria
Nabão
Ferreira do Zêzere
Proe a-N
Nazaré
Batalha
Vila Nova de Ourém
Vila de R
Barragem do Castelo de Bod
Alcobaça
A
Fátima
Tomar
B

AVEIRO ✪

The 'Venice of Portugal' sits on the edge of the great Ria and is sliced through by three canals, each spanned by arched bridges. Aveiro's wealth was in fishing, salt-panning and the gathering of *moliço* water weed – a rich, natural fertiliser. The brightly painted *moliceiro* boats with high, curved bows are of Phoenician ancestry and although chemical fertilisers have taken much of the trade, *molico* is still a prized natural resource, gathered with long rakes. By the late 16th century the town was an important port, but gradually declined as the coastal sand banks closed the lagoon's sea mouth. In 1808, the sandbar was breached with explosives and the traditional industries were rekindled, though never to their earlier level.

Above: *a moliceiro seaweed-gathering boat*

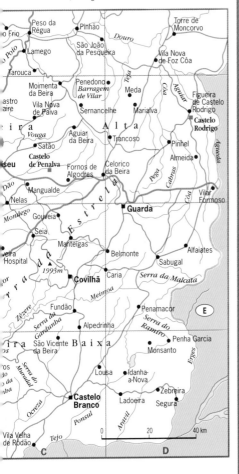

Above: *the tiled façade of a typical Aveiro house*

Aveiro

✚ 36A3

✉ 52km south of Porto

ℹ Tourist Office: Rua João Mendonça 8 (☎ 234 424 680)

❓ Aveiro holds a major festival at the end of August (dates variable), with *moliceiro* boat races

⊞ 30B2
✉ 20km west of Braga
ℹ Tourist Office: Largo da
Porta Nova (☎ 253
811882)
❓ As well as the Thursday
market, there is a major
religious festival, the
Festa das Cruces, on
3 May

BARCELOS ●●●

Barcelos stages the largest weekly agricultural fair and market in the north of Portugal. Bartering begins at dawn every Thursday in the expansive Campo da República square which, from Friday to Wednesday, appears out of all proportion to this small, rural town. By mid-morning Barcelos is a riot of trading with crates of chickens and rabbits; truckfuls of cattle, sheep and pigs; crude pottery including the famous cocks in dozens of different sizes, and cherubic-looking monks dressed in black robes with strings attached which, when pulled, may shock the

The Festa das Cruces *in Barcelos is one of many festivals that erupt across the Minho in summer*

unsuspecting; huge piles of fruit and vegetables; cassettes whose vendors try to blast each other out of contention with tinny decks running on car batteries; and clothes ranging from rustic berets to real leather bomber jackets.

The town is worth a brief stop on non-market days to see the enormous square centred by a beautiful fountain.

⊞ 30B2
✉ 52km northeast of Porto
ℹ Tourist Office: Avenida
da Liberdade 1 (☎ 253
262550)

BRAGA ●●

Braga is sometimes known as the 'Portuguese Rome'. The town is the religious capital of Portugal. At times during Portuguese history, the Church has wielded more power than the monarchy or government with Braga at the centre of this influence. Since the revolution of 1974 the ecclesiastic and political establishments have had less to do with each other, but Portugal is still a strongly spiritual nation and Braga's Holy Week celebrations in particular

(➤ 116) are a striking testament to the depth of religious feeling here.

There are 80 churches in this town, of which only the **Sé (Cathedral)** is unmissable. The foundations are 12th-century, with the main west door and the whole southern portal the most obvious visible survivors of the original Romanesque buildings. There are Gothic, Renaissance, baroque and Manueline amongst an extraordinary diversity of styles which somehow come together into a harmonious whole. Most striking is a pair of ornate gilt 18th-century organs adorned with cherubs, dolphins

Braga's Cathedral interior is an extraordinary hotch-potch of styles

and mermaids. In the Capela de São Pedro (St Peter's Chapel) are some outstanding *azulejos* by the master tile artist António Oliveira Bernardes; also not to be missed is a beautiful fresco of the Virgin in the Gothic Capela de São Geraldo (St Gerald's Chapel) and the Capela dos Reis (Chapel of the Kings) containing the tombs of Dom Henriques and Dona Teresa, whose son, Dom Afonso Henriques, became the first king of Portugal.

The pick of Braga's other sites are the Capela dos Coimbras (Coimbras Chapel) on Rua do Soto with its flamboyant Manueline tower and, inside, *azulejos* depicting the story of Adam and Eve; the splendid 17th-century baroque Igreja Santa Cruz (Holy Cross Church) on Rua do Anjo; and the extensive Antigo Paço Espiscopal (former Archbishop's Palace) with its peaceful, well-tended Santa Barbara gardens and Largo do Paco courtyard.

Three kilometres outside Braga is an ornate baroque terraced staircase of more than 1,000 steps leading up to the Bom Jesus sanctuary.

Driving Tour of The Douro Valley

Distance
About 330km

Time
Ten hours, including stops

Start point
Low Level, Dom Luis I Bridge, Porto
 33B1

End point
Porto city centre
 33B1

Lunch
Pousada Barão de Forrester (€€€)
✉ Alijó

Hydro-electric dams have transformed the Douro into a series of long, anguine lakes

From the lower level of the Dom Luis bridge, meander up the north bank of the river, passing two dams, before arriving at Peso da Régua.

Régua (as it is signposted, and always known) is one of the main port-producing cities, although it offers little to see or do. Better to continue on through the increasingly wild and spectacular scenery.

Cross the road bridge to the south bank of the Douro. From here, a beautiful route follows the river, which is turned into a long, serpentine lake by a huge hydro-electric dam. An iron bridge crosses the river at Pinhão.

Pinhão is a small town at the heart of the port-producing country. The red-tiled roofs of long, barrel warehouses are, as in Vila Nova de Gaia, whitewashed with the familiar names of the great port-shipping companies. The town itself, however, has little to detain the visitor, other than some beautiful *azulejo* tiles on the station platform, depicting traditional Douro rural life.

Another spectacular road twists up the valley of the Pinhão tributary, through dramatic, rocky scenery with mountainsides carved into terraces of vineyards, olive groves and citrus orchards which have been hewn and blasted out of the rock. This road leads up to the small town of Alijó. From here, take the road to Populo, to join the main IP4 Porto/Braganza highway. Pull off the IP4 at the Vila Real signpost, and follow signposts to Sabrosa and Solar de Mateus, which is 3km south of the town.

Solar De Mateus is a splendid, 18th-century palace famous the world over for gracing the label of every bottle of Mateus Rosé sold. There is no other particular connection between between the palace and the wine, so don't expect a tasting. A tour of the treasure-filled palace and beautiful grounds, however, is a treat.

Turn off the IP4 at the Amarante signpost, to explore this lovely town (▶ 36). Re-join the IP4 (now a motorway) to return to central Porto. There is a toll to pay before you reach the city.

BRAGANÇA (BRAGANZA) ✪✪

Up in the extreme northeast of the country and cut off from the rest of Portugal by three mountain ranges, Bragança stands isolated. Yet behind this remoteness is a city with an illustrious past: it has been fought over from prehistoric times through to the 19th-century Peninsular War, with sieges, battles and invasions turning on control of the walled citadel and its massive grey stone ramparts. The dukedom of Bragança became the royal house of Portugal, and supplied England with a queen, when Charles II married Catherine of Bragança.

There are bustling fruit, vegetable and grain markets distracting attention from the stately churches and fading, grandiose buildings of another era. Steep cobbled lanes lead up to the gates of the citadel and castle walls, within which everyday life goes on around the soaring Gothic keep. Washing hangs drying outside cottages with red-tiled roofs, haphazardly thrown together. Children play and chickens scratch about the vegetable plots and rubbish heaps, creating an almost medieval atmosphere.

Bragança is dominated by its forbidding and seemingly impenetrable castle. A tall keep is surrounded by crenellated turrets, with only narrow slits letting in any light. Fittingly, it houses a Military Museum charting the history of Portugal at war, with emphasis on the African colonies. From a platform at the top of the keep, there are wonderful views over the town and mountains.

🞣 31E3
✉ 253km northeast of Porto
ℹ Tourist Office: Avenida Cidade de Zamora (☎ 273 381273)
🍽 Many cafés and restaurants in the lower town

Castle and Military Museum
🕐 Fri–Wed 9–12, 2–5. Closed public holidays
♿ None
💰 Cheap

Above: *the forbidding citadel at Bragança has been fortified since prehistoric times*

Did you know ?

Catherine of Bragança married English King Charles II. Her dowry included the Portuguese trading post of Bombay, and she introduced to England the custom of taking afternoon tea.

✚ 36B2

✉ 150km northeast of Lisbon

ℹ️ Tourist Office: Largo da Portagem (☎ 239 855930)

University buildings

🕐 Mon–Sat 9:30–12, 2–5; library 9:30–12, 2–5. Closed Sun and public holidays

Monastery of the Holy Cross

✉ Praça 8 de Maio

🕐 Daily 8:30–12:30, 2–6:30

Conimbriga ruins

✉ 17km south of Coimbra, off the N1

🕐 May–Sep daily 9–8; Oct–Apr 9–1, 2–6. Museum 10–1, 2–6

COIMBRA ●●●

Set on a steep hill rising from the north bank of the River Mondego, Coimbra is one of the oldest university towns in Europe. It was also the capital of Portugal in the 12th and 13th centuries, after Guimarães and before Lisbon. Curiously, however, this concentration of historic buildings, romantically set on a hill overlooking the river, makes few concessions to tourism. The atmosphere varies between lively and youthful in term time, and stuffy and museum-like during vacations.

The **Velha Universidade (Old University)** of Coimbra was founded in 1290. Up at the highest point of the city is the institution's main courtyard, enclosed by a great ceremonial hall with a superb, 17th-century painted ceiling; the gloriously flamboyant, Manueline São Miguel chapel; and a small Museum of Sacred Art. The most splendid building in Coimbra, however, is the university library, which is composed of three glittering 18th-century baroque rooms with vast expanses of gilded wood. These have many oriental features, reflecting the Age of Discoveries.

The **Sé Velha (the Old Cathedral)** is a beautiful Romanesque church with many more recent features, begun in the late 12th century after Coimbra had become capital of the new Kingdom of Portugal. There is a beautiful altarpiece and some fine Renaissance side chapels, but

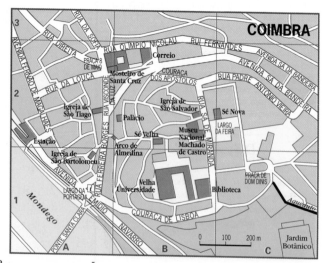

somehow it is the deeply moving ambience of the cathedral which is the true attraction.

Down in the 'new' town is Coimbra's other great architectural jewel, the **Mosteiro da Santa Cruz (Monastery of the Holy Cross)**. Like the cathedral, it was founded in the 12th century by Afonso Henriques, first king of Portugal, since when it has been liberally endowed with embellishments. The most interesting features are the ornate, carved stone pulpit in the centre of the church; the Manueline choir, where the voyages of Vasco da Gama are depicted in gilt wood carvings; and the sacristy where there is a collection of Renaissance art including a number of works by Grão Vasco (➤ 47).

Seventeen kilometres south of Coimbra, is **Conimbriga**, the largest Roman archaeological site in Portugal. Disappointingly, less than a quarter of the site has been excavated, but it is worth visiting to see the superb mosaic floors that survive.

Above: *Coimbra's glittering university library*
Right: *the 13th-century university, one of the oldest in Europe*

➕ 36A2
✉ 42km west of Coimbra
ℹ Tourist Office: Avenida
25 de Abril (☎ 233
422610)

FIGUEIRA DA FOZ ✪

Figueira da Foz is a fishing port and small beach holiday resort at the mouth of the River Mondego. The chief attraction is the enormous beach, ½km wide; the great Atlantic breakers are popular with surfers, although the rough sea can disappoint families who come hoping to swim. The town has several modern holiday hotels, discos, a casino and tennis courts.

➕ 30B2
✉ 49km northeast of Porto
and 22km southeast of
Braga
ℹ Tourist Offices: Alameda
de São Damaso (☎ 253
412450) and Praça de
Santiago (☎ 253 518790)

Castle
🕑 Daily 9–12:30, 2:30–5:30

Paço dos Duques
☎ 253 412273
🕑 Daily 9:30–12:30, 2–5:30
♿ None
💰 Oct–May cheap; Jun–Sep
moderate; free Sun AM

GUIMARÃES ✪✪

In 1139 Afonso Henriques was declared the first king of Portugal, and made Guimarães his capital. Although the centre of power soon shifted south – first to Coimbra and later to Lisbon – Guimarães still has a historic kernel, reached beyond the sprawl of textile and shoe factories which make it an important and prosperous industrial centre.

The ruined 10th-century **castle** stands rather dramatically on a rocky hill in the middle of town. There are seven great towers surrounding the keep, but otherwise little to see other than the great views over Guimarães and the surrounding countryside from the ramparts, which can be easily climbed.

The **Paço dos Duques (Palace of the Dukes of Braganza)** is the principal monument and museum to Guimarães's status as the cradle of the Portuguese nation. A fine, bronze statue of Afonso Henriques stands outside, guarding the four sturdy buildings with massive corner towers, built by Dom Afonso, the first Duke of Bragança. Inside, the unmissable rooms are the banqueting hall with its splendid wooden ceiling, and a fine collection of Persian carpets and Flemish tapestries.

LUSO 😊😊

The still, fresh mineral water of the famous Luso spa is favoured all over Portugal. It has a high level of radio-activity, which may sound alarming but is, apparently, beneficial. Certainly, many Portuguese regard the waters of Luso as a panacea; liver complaints in particular are reported to be eased at the very mention of a drop of Luso water. The Buçaco Palace Hotel (▶ 100) once described itself in a brochure as 'the shadiest hotel in Portugal'. This was actually a reference to the hotel's beautiful 100ha walled forest of oak, cork, pine and rare imported exotic trees (which do indeed throw a deep shade) with walkways and streams.

SERRA DO CARAMULO 😊😊

Caramulo is the main town in the Serra do Caramulo, a range of rolling inland mountains little visited by foreign tourists, but an excellent stop for motorists taking a hinterland route between north and south. The town of Caramulo itself is on the edge of the Cambarinho Natural Park, in which rare forms of oleander are conserved, amid vineyards and cattle pasture. The town has a small *pousada* (▶ 103) and two unlikely museums – one housing a collection of vintage cars, the other 'Ancient and Modern Art' including works by Dali and Picasso.

SERRA DA ESTRÊLA (▶ 24, TOP TEN)

➕ 36B2
✉ 25km northeast of Coimbra
ℹ Tourist Office: Rua Emídio Navarro (☎ 231 939133)

Opposite: *Figueira da Foz attracts wind-surfers and board-surfers alike*

➕ 36B3
✉ Caramulo is 40km southwest of Viseu

Museu de Arte
☎ 232 861270
🕐 Daily 10–1, 2–6
💰 Expensive

Below: *Caramulo boasts Portugal's finest collection of vintage cars*

<!-- sidebar -->
🚩 30B3

✉ 52km north of Viana do Castelo and 108km north of Porto

🕐 Unrestricted access to the walls

ℹ Tourist Office: Avenida de Espanha (☎ 251 23374)

🚩 30A2

✉ 56km north of Porto

ℹ Tourist Office: Praça de Erva (☎ 258 822620)

❓ Viana stages northern Portugal's greatest *romaria* and *festa*, Nossa Senhora da Agonía, over the weekend nearest to 15 August

Above: *sweeping views over Viana do Castelo and the Minho coast from the basilica of Santa Luzia*

VALENÇA DO MINHO ✪✪

Looking across the Minho towards Tuy, its Spanish counterpart, the border town of Valença do Minho has for centuries been on Portugal's front line of defence. Two massive sets of ramparts protect the old town which is entered via a drawbridge; inside are narrow cobbled streets and a lively atmosphere with large numbers of shops, patronised by Spaniards who have crossed the frontier to sniff out the best bargains. There are great views across to Spain from the walls, which can be walked around, and from the *pousada* (► 103) set into the ramparts. The new town, at the bottom of the hill outside the walls, has little of interest.

VIANA DO CASTELO ✪✪✪

This attractive fishing port, and venue for the greatest *festa* in the north of Portugal each August, stands on the north bank of the Lima estuary, dominated by the lusciously wooded Santa Luzia mountain. The beautiful Praça da República is surrounded by fine houses decorated with Manueline embellishments dating from the 16th and 17th centuries, when the town became prosperous on trade and fishing for *bacalhau* (dried salt cod) from the Grand Banks of Newfoundland, and exporting wine to Britain.

Viana is a delightful town to wander around and has a strong folkloric tradition; on Sundays and saints' days, people are frequently to be seen on the streets wearing traditional regional dress – the women in long embroidered skirts and veils, the men in bright waistcoats and black, broad-brimmed hats.

A narrow 4km road winds up to the basilica and hotel on Monte de Santa Luzia, from where the views over the north of Portugal are sensational. On a clear day the coastline can be traced from the Minho and Spain beyond, most of the way down to Porto.

VISEU ⚫⚫

Viseu is a solemn town of dignified airs at the heart of Dão wine-producing country. Its history is centred on Vasco Fernandes (1480–1543), later styled Grão Vasco – the 'Great Vasco' – founder of the Viseu school of painting. As he was one of the most eminent painters in Portuguese history, and the one principally responsible for introducing the Renaissance to the country, his adopted home town, Viseu, is naturally proud of him. So there is a Grão Vasco museum, a Grão Vasco hotel, and Grão Vasco wine – one of the most famous brands of Dão.

The **Grão Vasco Museum** is housed in the Bishop's Palace opposite the Cathedral. Many of Grão Vasco's most famous works are exhibited, including his interpretations of St Peter and St Sebastian. The museum also contains work by Gaspar Vaz, another Portuguese master, and some beautiful 16th-century *azulejos*.

The twin-towered Cathedral was built in a hotch-potch of different styles, between the 13th and 18th-centuries, and is worth seeing. Most remarkable are the gilded, baroque altarpiece, and the Renaissance cloisters, decorated with 18th-century *azulejos*.

🞧 37C3
✉ 81km southeast of Porto
ℹ Tourist Office: Avenida Calouste Gulbenkian (☎ 232 420950)

Grão Vasco Museum
☎ 232 26249
🕐 Tue–Sun 9:30–12:30, 2–5. Closed public holidays
♿ Few
✋ Moderate. Free Sun

A medieval pillory still stands outside Viseu's imperious Cathedral

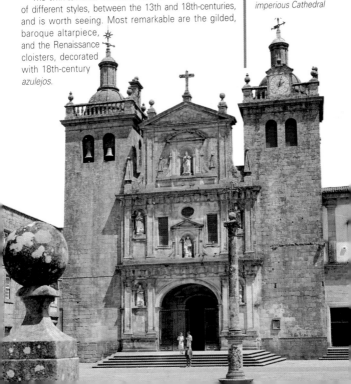

Lisbon & Central Portugal

As Portugal's capital city, Lisbon holds a concentration of historical and cultural attractions and is the nation's most cosmopolitan city by far. Standing roughly halfway between north and south, it is also strategically placed for exploring the central regions of Estremadura and Ribatejo.

Estremadura is a region of rocky coast and flat plains, flanked by gentle hills to the north and south, and sprinkled with historic towns such as Sintra and Alcobaça.

The Ribatejo region to the northwest of Lisbon is less culturally rich. However, as it encompasses the flood-plain of the Tagus, its fecundity lies in the alluvial soil, allowing wheat and rice to be grown, and horses and cattle to graze on fertile pastures. The only place of great historical note in Ribatejo is Tomar, where the Order of Christ, successors of the crusading Knights Templar, had their base.

' Porto works and
Braga prays,
Coimbra studies but
Lisbon plays. '

PORTUGUESE
APHORISM

Left: *Campo de Santa Clara, Lisbon*

49

Lisbon

In a country with a reputation for melancholy, Lisbon is proud to call itself the national playground as well as the nation's capital. As a laid-back and attractive city, it makes an excellent short-break destination for tourists.

If you are fit, the steep gradients of the hills over which central Lisbon is scattered are best explored on foot. The most famous part of town is the Alfama district, a labyrinth of cobbled alleys, miniature squares and whitewashed houses, rising in tiers from the Tagus.

The architectural contrast with the nearby, low-lying Baixa district, which was totally destroyed in the devastating earthquake of 1755, is dramatic. This area was rebuilt in precise grid form with magnificent squares and avenues.

Another district which attracts visitors to Lisbon is the Bairro Alto. This is the most bohemian quarter of the city, rising to the west in steep streets and stone staircases, and lined with restaurants, *fado* houses and mildly raffish bars. The lower part of the district, from where several lifts rise to the upper reaches, is the elegant Chiado, with fashionable department stores and tea houses. The area is being painstakingly restored after a serious fire in 1988.

Westwards along the Tagus, the other area of Lisbon not to be missed is Belém. The suburb is home to some of Lisbon's finest Manueline architecture, evoking Portugal's great era of world discovery.

Dom José presides over Lisbon's splendid Praça do Comércio

What to See in Lisbon

CASTELO DE SÃO JORGE YOLISIPÓNIA

Crowning a hill surrounded by the Alfama district, the castle is built on 5th-century Visigoth and 9th-century Moorish foundations. The present 12th–14th-century edifice was begun by Afonso Henriques, following his capture of Lisbon from the Moors in 1147. A climb up through the Alfama district to the top is rewarded by stupendous views over the Tagus and its suspension bridge, and by beautiful gardens planted when the castle was restored in 1938.

MOSTEIRO DOS JERÓNIMOS (➤ 21, TOP TEN)

MUSEU CALOUSTE GULBENKIAN (➤ 22, TOP TEN)

MUSEU DA MARINHA (MARITIME MUSEUM)

This is the place to go if you want to understand how, in the 15th and 16th centuries, Portugal rose to become one of the greatest maritime and trading powers on earth. The museum houses maps, documents, navigational instruments and models of ships from the era of discoveries through to this century. There is also an interesting section on naval aviation.

> ### Did you know ?
>
> *The anguished, wailing songs beloved of the Portuguese belong to a musical tradition known as* fado. *The word means* fate, *and is unique to Portugal. It expresses the national sense of longing, left behind when the nation's sense of greatness evaporated.*

➕ 53D3
🕐 Daily 9–6
🚌 Bus 37, tram 12, 28
♿ Few
🎫 Free

➕ Off map 52A1
✉ Praça do Imperio
☎ 21 362 0019
🕐 Tue–Sun 10–5. Closed public holidays
🚌 Buses from the Baixa district, tram 15
♿ Few
🎫 Cheap. Free Sun

Above: *the Castelo de São Jorge crowns the Alfama district, and has wide views over the Baixa and beyond*

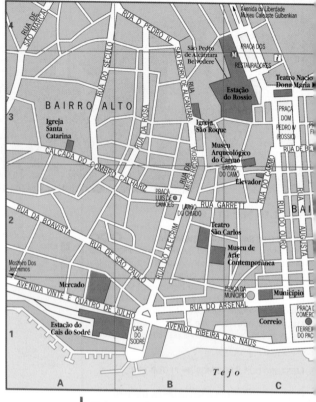

Off map 52A1

Praça Afonso de Albuquerque, Belém

Tue–Sun 10–6. Closed public holidays

Buses from the Baixa district, tram 15

Moderate. Free Sun

Few

Off map 53

Esplanada D Carlos 1, Parque dos Nações

21 891 7002

Daily 10–7 (until 6 Nov–Mar)

Oriente

Expensive

MUSEU DOS COCHES (COACH MUSEUM)

Immediately to the east of the Presidential Palace at Belém, in a former riding school, is this superb collection of horse-drawn coaches. The collection spans three centuries and comes from royal households around Europe including Portugal, Spain, France and Italy.

Some are extravagant and ornate – glittering with gold and lined with velvet. Pride of place goes to a sumptuous trio of coaches built in Rome for the Portuguese ambassador to the Vatican, the better to project an image of Portugal as a proud and wealthy nation.

OCEANARIO

This spectacular oceanarium in the Parque das Nações (Park of the Nations) was designed by Peter Chermayett and is the largest in Europe. It opened in 1998 as the centrepiece of the Expo '98 world exposition and has become one of Lisbon's most popular visitor attractions. It features a huge central tank (the largest in Europe), with four others around it, representing the world's oceans.

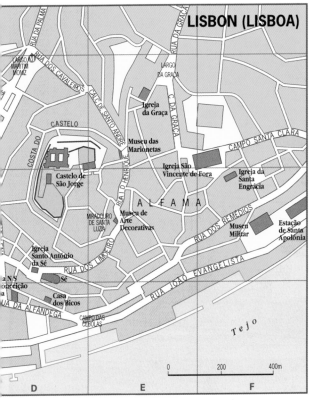

LISBON (LISBOA)

D   E   F

0   200   400m

PADRÃO DOS DESCOBRIMENTOS ✪ (MONUMENT TO THE DISCOVERIES)

This huge, triumphalist monument was unveiled in 1960 to mark the 500th anniversary of Prince Henry the Navigator's death. Curved to the seaward side and angular on the other, it also represents a ship's prow, and serves as a memorial to all players in the Portuguese Age of Discoveries. A lift whisks you to the top, from where there are views over the city: the Tagus estuary spanned by the great 25 de Abril suspension bridge to the west, and the new Vasco da Gama bridge to the east.

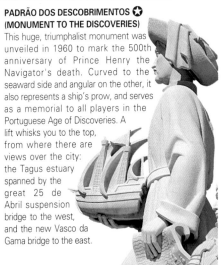

➕ Off map 52A1
✉ Belém
🕐 Tue–Sun 9–6:30
🚌 Buses from the Baixa district, tram 15
♿ Good
🎫 Moderate

Prince Henry the Navigator gazes across the Tagus from the Monument to the Discoveries

53

Off map 52A1
Calcada da Ajuda
Tours: Thu–Tue 10–5
Tram 18 from Baixa, or
Bus 14, 43, 60 from
Belém
Few
Moderate

52C1

PALÁCIO DA AJUDA

Above the pink National Palace of Belém, the official residence of the president of Portugal (not open to the public), is the former Ajuda royal palace, built between 1796 and 1826. It was occupied by the royal family on their return from exile in Brazil, and remained the royal residence until the abolition of the monarchy in 1910.

It is sumptuously furnished with tapestries, sculpture, oriental carpets and historic paintings, and has displays of royal jewellery, crystal and other treasures. The palace is still used for state occasions such as banquets for visiting royalty.

PRACA DO COMÉRCIO
(Also known by its old name TERREIRO DO PAÇO)

The most splendid of Lisbon's many squares built after the 1755 earthquake is in the centre, giving on to the Tagus, and is lined on three sides with imperious classical façades, most of which are now government buildings.

Left: *Lisbon's Cathedral interior tells the story of Portuguese architecture*
Below: *the Torre de Belém*

SÉ (CATHEDRAL) ✪✪

Like many Portuguese cathedrals, including those at Porto, Évora and the Sé Velha at Coimbra, Lisbon's cathedral was originally a fortress as well as a place of worship. Sturdy twin crenellated towers, rising above the façade, are testimony to this. It was founded in the 12th century following the conquest of the Moors and, from the outside, maintains a distinct Romanesque mien.

The interior tells a fuller story of Portuguese architectural history. The nave is in plain, somewhat austere Romanesque style, but the ambulatory and lancet windows are Gothic. There is a beautiful baroque crib and a fine 17th-century organ.

A side chapel houses the tombs and stone effigies of notables including archbishops of Lisbon and Lopo Fernandes Pacheco, a 14th-century comrade-in-arms of King Afonso IV, with a dog at his feet. Off this chapel are the 13th-century monastic cloisters. A door from the south transept leads into the sacristy, where treasures and religious art are displayed in the Museu do Tesouro da Sé. Try not to miss the mother-of-pearl oriental casket, said to contain relics of St Vincent.

➕ 53D2
✉ Largo da Sé
🕐 Tue–Sat 9–7, Sun, Mon and public holidays 9–5
♿ Few
🎟 Church free; cloisters cheap. Free on Sun

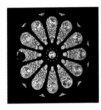

TORRE DE BELÉM ✪✪

This 16th-century fortress on the edge of the Tagus has defended the capital and housed political prisoners; today it is one of Lisbon's most photogenic landmarks, looking almost like a tall ship tethered to the quayside and floating serenely on the river.

Inside is a museum of weapons and armour, and you can climb up to the top of the tower for fine views over the Tagus estuary.

➕ Off map 52A1
✉ Avenida de Brasília
☎ 21 362 0034
🕐 Tue–Sun 10–4
🚌 Tram 15 from Baixa, bus 29, 43 from Belém
♿ None
🎟 Moderate

Lisbon Walk

Distance
3½km

Time
About three hours

Start point
Praça do Comércio
✛ 52C1

End point
Rua Garrett
✛ 52C2

Lunch
Cervejeria da Trindade (€€)
✉ 20 Rua da Trindade
(adjacent to Largo do
Carmo)

Start at the Praça do Comércio.

This is Lisbon's bustling centre, also frequently called by its old name Terreiro do Paço, after the royal palace which stood here until its destruction in the 1755 earthquake. It is set on the river with the Castelo Sâo Jorge towering above.

Follow the long, straight, pedestrianised Rua Augusta away from the river. There is frequently an almost carnival atmosphere along here, with street performers and vendors selling flowers, roasted chestnuts and lottery tickets. The road runs into Rossio Square.

Rossio Square is lined with cafés spilling on to the pavement, aflutter with pigeons, and presided over by a statue of the playwright Gil Vincente adorning the façade of the Dona Maria II National Theatre. This is Lisbon at its liveliest; stop a while and watch the world go by.

Leave the square via Rua Áurea at the southwest corner. One block along is the iron-girdered Elevador Santa Justa. Take this lift up to the top for glorious views over the city. A bridge leads from the lift, into Rua do Carmo. On the right is the Convento do Carmo.

Wander around the atmospheric ruins of this Carmelite convent which tumbled down in the 1755 earthquake, and was never rebuilt. It is easy to forget that you are in the middle of the city.

Rossio Square in Lisbon's Baixa district, an ideal place to sit and watch the world go by

Cross to the other side of the Largo do Carmo, turn left into Rua Serpa Pinto, and left again into Rua Garrett.

Named after author Almeida Garrett, this is one of Lisbon's most fashionable and characterful streets. On the left, at number 20, is the famous A Brasileira. This gilt and mirrored coffee house, with a bronze statue of poet Fernando Pessoa outside, simply oozes atmosphere. It has long been a haunt of Lisbon's literary circle.

What to See in Central Portugal

ALCOBAÇA (▶ 16, TOP TEN)

BATALHA (▶ 17, TOP TEN)

CASCAIS ✪✪

Cascais is a smart, large and still-burgeoning holiday resort, surpassed in size on the Lisbon coast only by Estoril. It is also a commuter town for wealthy Lisboetas. Echoing the story of so many fishing ports, especially in the Algarve, the centre of activity is now the tourist trade, with scores of hotels and restaurants, but catches are still unloaded daily on the beach and auctioned in the local market.

➕ 58A1
✉ 32km west of Lisbon and 13km from Sintra
ℹ Tourist Office: Rua Visconde da Luz (☎ 21 484 4086)

ESTORIL ✪✪

Portugal's most popular holiday resort north of the Algarve was famous long before the 1960s tourist explosion. Since the end of the 19th century the town has attracted the rich and famous from around Europe, and in the 1940s and 1950s became home to various deposed crowned heads, such as King Humberto of Italy and King Juan of Spain.

Some imposing façades and the casino recall this era, although the other facilities are as up-to-date as anywhere. This combination of an old-fashioned holiday ambience and the new cosmopolitan image, gives Estoril an atmosphere which is the antithesis of quaint. On warm weekends, and particularly during the summer holidays, you'll find the town bustling as wealthy Lisboetas flock to enjoy the beaches and the wealth of excellent restaurants for a long lazy lunch or dinner.

➕ 58A1
✉ 29km from Lisbon
ℹ Tourist Office: Arcadas do Parque (☎ 21 466 3813; www.estorilcoast-tourism.com)

Café society in the smart resort of Cascais, on the Lisbon coast

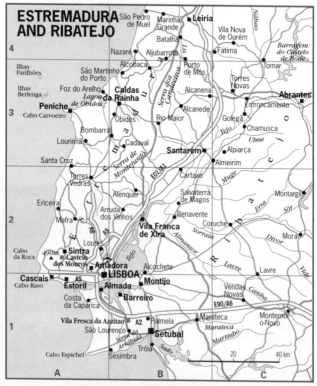

ESTREMADURA AND RIBATEJO

São Pedro de Muel · Marinha Grande · **Leiria**
Batalha
Vila Nova de Ourém · *Nabão*
4
Nazaré · Aljubarrota
Barragem do Castelo de Bode
Alcobaça
Fátima
Porto de Mós
Tomar
Ilhas Farilhões
São Martinho do Porto
Torres Novas
Ilhas Berlenga
Foz do Arelho · **Caldas da Rainha**
Alcanena
Abrantes
Lagoa de Óbidos
Alcanede
Entroncamento
Peniche
Cabo Carvoeiro
Óbidos
Rio Maior
Golegã
Chamusca
3
Bombarral
Tejo
Ulme
Lourinhã
Cadaval
Santarém
Alpiarça
Santa Cruz
Almeirim
Torres Vedras
Cartaxo
Muge
Alenquer
Salvaterra de Magos
Montargil
2
Ericeira
Arruda dos Vinhos
Benavente
Coruche
Erra
Mafra
Vila Franca de Xira
Mora
Sorraia
Divor
Loures
Tejo
Cabo da Roca
Sintra · Castelo dos Mouros
Amadora
Alcochete
Lavre
Lavre
Cascais
Cabo Raso
Estoril
LISBOA
Montijo
Vendas Novas
Canha
Vide
Almada
Costa da Caparica
Barreiro
E90/A6
Vila Fresca da Azeitão
Pálmela
Marateca
Montemor-o-Novo
1
São Lourenço
Serra da Arrábida
Setúbal
Marateca
Martinho
Cabo Espichel
Sesimbra
Tróia
Sado
0   20   40 km

A   B   C

Arrábida Coastal Drive

Leave Lisbon via the 2km–long 25 de Abril suspension bridge, leaving the IP1 motorway at the second exit and following the N378 to Santana. Turn right here, onto the N379 to Cabo Espichel.

Cabo Espichel is a desolate, wind-fretted cape at the furthest end of a barren plateau. It has a raw beauty to it as you look out over towering, sea-battered cliffs.

Return to Santana, and turn right, twisting down for a couple of kilometres to Sesimbra.

Sesimbra is an attractive fishing port, though its popularity has brought mass tourist development on the surrounding hills.

Return to Santana and take the 397 again heading east. After 8kms turn right at signs for Portinho da Arrábida, into the Parque Naturel de Arrábida.

The road leads through vineyards and orchards before climbing into the Serra da Arrábida hills.

After 10kms the road splits. Signs for Portinho da Arrábida lead right, down to the south coast where there are excellent beaches, but take the left fork and the road travels along the spine of the Serra da Arrábida with outstanding views south to the flat peninsula of the Costa da Gaié and the Sado Estuary. Once the road descends, at the T-junction turn left (signposted Lisbon and Azietão) to reach the village of Vila Nogueira da Azietão.

This attractive inland village is headquarters of the Fonseca wine. Here you can visit the historic cellars and taste the latest wines 'en primeur'.

Distance/time
75km; 6 hours including stops

Start point
25 de Abril Bridge
✚ 58A1

End point
Vila Nogueira da Azietão
✚ 58B1

Lunch
Nova Fortaleza (€€)
✉ Largo dos Bombaldes, Sesimbra

Above: *Sesimbra's fishing fleet lands fresh, deep-water fish and sea food*

Opposite: *ready for picking? A wine-maker inspects the grapes before the wine harvest in the Ribatejo*

FÁTIMA

Fátima is one of the principal places of pilgrimage in the Roman Catholic world. On 13 May 1917 three peasant children saw a vision of the Virgin Mary speaking to them from the top of an oak tree. She warned of cataclysmic events about to take place in Russia, and pleaded for prayer and sacrifice as prerequisites for peace in the world. Further apparitions took place on the 13th day of each subsequent month, culminating in an inexplicable spectacle on 13 October, when 70,000 onlookers saw the sun spinning like a ball in the sky. Many of these witnesses are still alive. Two of the children died soon afterwards but the third, Sister Lucia, still lives as an enclosed Carmelite nun.

The phenomenon sparked a spiritual regeneration in Portugal. Millions visit the site every year, including upwards of 100,000 on 13 May and 13 October. A basilica has been built on the spot of the apparitions with a vast tarmac area where the faithful gather. There are dozens of cheap hotels and hundreds of stalls selling tawdry religious artefacts.

Fátima has nothing for the sceptical. Others find a source of spiritual energy here.

- 58C4
- ✉ 20km east of Batalha
- ℹ Tourist Office: Avenida José Alves Correia da Silva (☎ 249 531139)

LEIRIA

Leiria is a pleasant little agricultural town on the River Liz, clustering around a perpendicular rock topped by a forbidding medieval castle. Inside a ring of defensive walls, is the sheer keep and the royal palace containing a vast hall. At night, the castle is floodlit and shines out like a beacon for miles around.

- 58B4
- ✉ 67km south of Coimbra
- ℹ Tourist Office: Jardim Luís de Camões (☎ 244 848770)

Castle
- 🕐 Mon–Fri 9–5:30/6:30, Sat–Sun 10–5:30/6:30
- ♿ None 🏷 Cheap

ÓBIDOS (► 23, TOP TEN)

SANTARÉM

The capital of the Ribatejo region is a bustling town on the west bank of the Tagus, which serves as the agricultural hub for the fertile outlying plains. These days Santarém is best known for being the bullfighting and dressage capital of Portugal. Fine specimens of both bulls and horses are to be seen grazing in the rich pastures surrounding the town – horsemanship was developed as a means of fighting the bulls by mounted *cavaleiros*.

However, Santarém is not a place to linger, unless you happen to be there during the last week in October or first week in November (it differs from year to year), when the great National Gastronomic Fair is held, and you can wander from stall to stall tasting regional titbits from all over Portugal, amid fireworks and jollity.

- 58B3
- ✉ 78km northeast of Lisbon
- ℹ Tourist Office: 63 Rua de Capelo Ivens (☎ 243 391512)
- ❓ National Gastronomic Fair in Oct/Nov (dates variable)

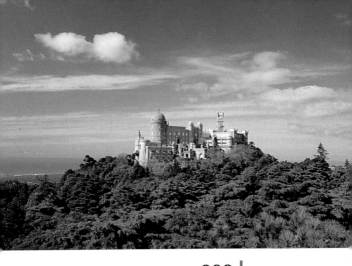

SINTRA ✪✪✪

High on a hilltop and surrounded by dense, green forests, Sintra has inspired poets as diverse as Camões and Byron, during centuries of its fashionability among writers, artists, musicians and European high society. The town was a summer retreat for royalty up until the abolition of the monarchy in 1910. A leisurely saunter along the forest trails is highly recommended before any sightseeing.

So many different Portuguese monarchs added their own embellishments to the **Palácio Nacional** that the whole defies any architectural classification. The two wings added by Manuel II in the 16th century sit awkwardly with the main structure.

Inside, the palace tour takes you through an astonishing diversity of rooms – each one a folly of one king or another. In the Magpie Room are 136 magpies, each with a rose in its beak representing the ladies of the court, one of whom King Joao is said to have presented with a rose when Queen Philippa wasn't looking. A magpie stole the rose, drawing the Queen's attention to her husband's philandering, so the story goes.

In the hills of the Serra de Sintra that surround the town is the 8th-century Castelo dos Mouros with commanding views over Sintra and the National Palace, and the Palácio Nacional da Pena, built in the mid-18th century by Ferdinand, husband of Queen Maria II. The pastel coloured riot of towers, turrets and arches is truly neo-Gothic in style and holds a wealth of period furniture including vast tapestries.

✚ 58A2
✉ 28km northwest of Lisbon
ℹ Tourist Office: Praça da República (☎ 21 923 1157)
❓ Music festival each July (dates variable)

Palácio National

✉ Praça da República
☎ 21 910 6840
🕐 Daily 10–5:30 (last admission 5). Closed public holidays. Tours every 20 minutes
♿ Good
💷 Jun–Sep, moderate; Oct–May, cheap

Opposite: *Fátima*
Above: *the Palácio Nacional rises above the lush forests of Sintra*

Did you know ?

Portuguese bullfights are very different from their Spanish counterparts. For one thing, the bull is not killed in the ring. Instead, the emphasis is on horsemanship, with most of the fighting done from the backs of thoroughbred Lusitano horses. But the bull leaves the ring exhausted and often has to be killed anyway.

In the Know

If you only have a short time to visit Portugal, or would like to get a real flavour of the country, here are some ideas:

10
Ways To Be A Local

Have a flexible attitude towards time. The Portuguese are notoriously unpunctual.

Learn a few words of Portuguese and make a point of using them in shops, restaurants or with hotel staff.

Shake hands when introduced to someone, and then again each time you meet.

Hang out in a café, where much of the national life is played out.

Avoid comparing Portugal, or the Portuguese language, with Spain or Spanish. The Portuguese take pride in the contrast with their Iberian neighbours.

Be careful discussing current or recent Portuguese political events. These can arouse strong feelings.

Understand something about football. This can be a great ice-breaker.

Be prepared to eat and drink copiously, especially if you are being entertained by a local.

Respect the Roman Catholic religion, particularly with appropriate dress and behaviour at churches.

Be familiar with the rudiments of Portuguese history. Particularly the era when Portugal was a major world power.

10
Good Places To Have Lunch

Adega Regional Kilowatt (€), Rua 31 de Janeiro, Amarante. Artisan produced air-dried ham in country bread accompanied by *vinho verde* is all that this tiny rustic eatery serves. The perfect lunch!

Café Ingles (€), 11 Escalada do Castello, Silves. Elegant 1920s mansion, now a café, with a large terrace under the shadow of Silves cathedral. Good range of Portuguese and international snacks.

Jardim dos Frangos (€), Avenida Marginal, Cascais. Grilled chicken and sardines with fresh salad form the main menu items at this exceptional budget restaurant. Expect to queue but it's worth it.

Nicola (€), Praça Dom Pedro IV 26, Lisbon. A grand, old-fashioned café in Lisbon's Baixa district. Perfect for a snack as you watch the world go by.

Muralhas de Faro (€€€), 1–7 Rue e Beco do Repuso Faro. Beautiful restaurant set in the old city walls serving Alentejo and Morrocan dishes.

Pousada de São Filipe (€€€), Fortress São Filipe, Setúbal. The magnificent views from the terrace atop the fortress walls matches the food served at this most dramatic *pousada*.

Solar de Monsaraz (€€), 38 Rua Conde de Monsaraz, Monsaraz, Alentejo. The best place in town to sample some hearty Alentejo dishes.

Pousada de São Francisco (€€€), Beja. Feast on superbly

prepared Alentejo specialities in the old monastic refectory.

The café (€), on Burgau beach, Algarve, west of Praia de Luz. Be sure to try the excellent grilled sardines and tomato salad.

Paraíso da Montanha (€€), on the road from Monchique up to Foia, Algarve. Sensational views and excellent spicy chicken *piri-piri*.

Top Activities

Golf: Portugal is one of Europe's top golfing destinations. Top courses include Penina (☎ 282 420200) and Quinta do Lago (☎ 289 396002) in the Algarve.

Tennis: Portugal's top tennis schools are the David Lloyd Centre at Vilamoura, and the Jonathan Markson Centre at Praia da Luz.

Surfing: Best places are Figuera da Foz, the west coast of the Algarve and Guincho on the Lisbon coast.

Swimming: The Algarve has some of Europe's finest beaches, such as the beautiful Praia Dona Ana and Praia do Camilo. On the Arrábida coast, Sesimbra's beach takes some beating.

Walking: Best regions for hikers are the Penêda-Gerêz National Park in the far north, and the central Serra da Estrêla.

Horse riding: There are many riding centres in the Algarve, including one at Vilamoura (☎ 289 322675) and one at Quinta dos Amigos near Almansil (☎ 289 395269).

Big-game fishing: The Algarve is one of the few places in Europe where

you can fish shark and tuna. Centres at Portimão (☎ 282 25866) and Vilamoura (☎ 289 315666).

Sailing: Good facilities for boat hire at Vilamoura. Also, yacht clubs at Lagos, Ferragudo and Carvoeiro.

Painting: Courses are held at Quinta do Barranco da Estrada in the Alentejo (☎ 283 933901).

Water Parks: There are several on the Algarve, including 'The Big One' near Portimão, and 'Wet 'n' Wild' at Almansil.

Best Views

- Santa Luzia Basilica, Viana do Castelo
- Upper level of Dom Luis I bridge, Porto
- Casal dos Loivos, above Pinhão, Alto Douro
- Torre, in the Serra da Estrêla (mainland Portugal's highest mountain peak)
- Top of the Belém tower, Lisbon
- Cabo Espichel, at the tip of the Arrábida peninsula
- The dining room window of the Pousada da Rainha Santa Isabel at Estremoz
- Battlements of Monsaraz castle
- Cliffs directly above Praia do Camilo, near Lagos, Algarve
- Foia, above Monchique, Algarve

Best Beaches

- Caminha, on the River Minho Estuary, bordering Spain
- Ofir, at the mouth of the Cávado, Minho
- São Martinho do Porto, near Leiria
- Cascais, on the Lisbon coast
- Portinho, on the Arrábida coast
- Vila Nova de Milfontes, Alentejo
- Bordeira, Algarve west coast
- Praia do Camilo, near Lagos, Algarve
- Praia Tres Irmãos, near Portimão, Algarve
- Ilha de Tavira, Algarve

┿ 58C4

✉ 135km northeast of Lisbon

ℹ Tourist Office: Avenida Dr Candido Madureira (☎ 249 322427)

Convento de Cristo

🕐 Apr–Sep 9–6:30 (last admission 6); Oct–Mar 9–5:30 (last admission 5)

♿ None

💰 Oct–May, cheap; Jun–Sep, moderate

❓ Tomar's *Festa dos Tabuleiros* (Festival of the Trays), one of Portugal's most famous festivals, takes place every two years at the beginning of July (dates vary)

Above and right: *the Convento de Cristo at Tomar, once a stronghold of the Knights Templar*

TOMAR ✪✪✪

Tomar is the architectural jewel of the Ribatejo region and should not be missed by anybody with an interest in historic buildings. It is also a pleasant little town on the banks of the River Nabão with some good hotels and restaurants, making it an excellent place to tourers to stop for the night.

The immense, fortified, hilltop **Convento de Cristo (Convent of Christ)** dominates Tomar. Parts of the crenellated walls date from the 12th century, when it was a stronghold of the Knights Templar, the powerful military order founded to keep pilgrim routes open to the Holy Land during the Crusades, and answerable only to the Pope. After its disbandment by Pope Clement V in 1330, King Dinis created in its place the Order of the Knights of Christ, with its seat at Tomar.

TORRES VEDRAS ✪

The famous 'lines of Torres Vedras' feature prominently in Peninsular War textbooks. They consist of three rings, each of about 100 fortified hilltops, built in 1809–10 by the Anglo-Portuguese forces under Wellington, to defend Lisbon from Napoleon's armies. Some of the walls, ditches and gun emplacements are still intact and can be identified from the N8 road; a scramble up also guarantees a view over the bumpy hills to the next fortification in the line on either side.

The best place to see the remains of the lines is from a reconstructed fort which stands just outside the town of Torres Vedras. There is unrestricted access to the lines, 24 hours a day, all through the year.

➕ 58A2
✉ 34km south of Óbidos
ℹ Avenida 5 de Outubro
(☎ 261 314094)

The Lines
♿ None
✋ Free

Flamboyant flourishes, typical of Manueline architecture, reflect Portugal's great maritime exploits

Alentejo

Alentejo means, literally, 'beyond the Tagus' and is a great, sun-baked plain bordered to the east by a backbone of high craggy mountains and the wide Guadiana river, which together form a natural border with Spain. The glorious, historic towns have a sleepy feel to them which defies the pivotal roles they have all played in Portuguese history.

The region covers over a third of the total area of Portugal but is home to barely a tenth of the population, so the Alentejo has a slow, little-changing pace of life. Other than a scattering of superb *pousadas*, such as the converted national monuments in Évora and Estremoz, accommodation of a high standard is extremely scarce. For as long as this remains the case, the Alentejo can be expected to maintain its remote, arcane atmosphere and its treasures will remain undiscovered by mass tourism.

> *'The fields in these days of mid-June had the first golden ears of ripe corn... the scarlet of the poppies was laughing like the lips of ardent girls.'*

JOSÉ DE ALMEIDA
Travelling in the Alentejo (1870)

Left: *a street in Portalegre*

Évora

Évora crowns a gentle hill, rising from the sunbaked plains of the Alentejo, surrounded by expansive fields of wheat, olive groves and cork forest. Almost entirely enclosed within sturdy, 14th-century walls, it is the sort of place a sightseer's dreams are made of, and one of the great joys of travelling in Portugal.

Évora is almost a museum of Portuguese art and architecture in itself. So extensive is the collection of historic buildings, packed tightly together within massive, stone city walls, that in 1986 UNESCO declared Évora a World Heritage Site.

Top: *a figure of Atlas supporting the world on his shoulders adorns Nossa Senhora da Graça church in Évora*

Above: *restored Evoramonte castle crowns a hill between Évora and Estremoz*

Fittingly, one of the city's finest architectural treasures, the 15th-century Convento dos Lóios, can be enjoyed to the full by visitors. It has been imaginatively converted into a *pousada*, with guests staying in the old monastic cells and eating (meditatively or otherwise) in the dining room along two sides of the main cloister quadrangle. After dinner you can relax in the chapter house, now the lounge.

The many other points of interest can all be easily explored on foot, as you wander along cobbled streets lined with cafés, enlivened by the city's sizeable student population. By night, floodlights bathe the city in luminous green, making it look from afar like a giant glow-worm; this makes Évora a romantic place for an after-dinner stroll. The tourist office is on Praça do Giraldo (☎ 266 702671).

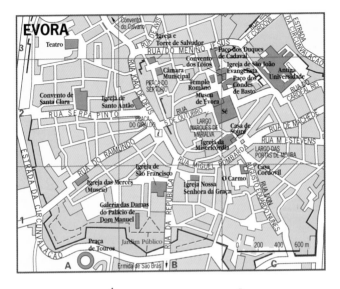

What to See in Évora

MUSEU DE ÉVORA 😊😊

The City Museum is housed in the ornate and well-proportioned 17th-century former palace of the Archbishops of Évora. Inside is one of the most eclectic collections of works of art in Portugal, ranging from Roman and medieval sculpture through 16th-century Flemish painting to modern art, where you can admire work by some of Portugal's foremost fine artists and sculptors.

The most famous exhibit, however, is the series of 13 powerfully expressive 14th-century panels portraying the Nascimento da Virgem (Birth of the Virgin), which was once part of the cathedral altarpiece.

➕ 69B2
☎ 266 22604
🕐 Closed for renovations, scheduled to reopen 2005 – call for times
♿ Few
🎟 Cheap

The Convento dos Lóis, now a magnificent pousada

+ 69B3
◷ Daily 10–12:30, 2–6
♿ Few
✋ Moderate

PAÇO DOS DUQUES DE CADAVAL
(PALACE OF THE DUKES OF CADAVAL)

A 14th-century palace up against the old city wall opposite the Convento dos Lóios monastery, crowned by a pair of fine and unmistakable crenellated towers. Inside there is a small art gallery exhibiting mainly portraits of bishops and other stuffy-looking ecclesiastics; it would all be rather dreary were it not for the exquisite painted ceiling, which is well worth going to see.

+ 69B1
✉ Rua da República
☎ 266 24521
◷ Mon–Sat 8:30–1, 2:30–6;
Sun 10–11:30, 2:30–6.
Closed at 5:30 during
May
♿ Few
💰 Main church free; Chapel
of Bones cheap

IGREJA DE SÃO FRANCISCO
(CHURCH OF ST FRANCIS)

Think carefully about whether you really want to see this one. Thousands of people do every year, on account of the famous Capela dos Ossos (Chapel of Bones); many leave revolted. The chapel, built by a macabre monk in the 15th century, is decorated with designs made from the bones of 5,000 human skeletons. There are skulls grinning at you from every direction, while at the far end of the chapel hang the shrivelled, leathery corpses of a man and a child. The smell of death seems to linger in the air, while an inscription in Portuguese translates menacingly as: 'We the bones lie in wait for yours'.

You reach the chapel through a chapterhouse where wax images of parts of the human body have been placed as votive offerings, by faithful pilgrims with ailments (the voluminous wax breasts are the petitions of infertile women). The braids of hair pinned to the wall at the chapel entrance are cut from brides, as an offering before their wedding.

Escape into the open air can be a welcome relief after this piece of sightseeing.

A window where the morbid can peer into Évora's gruesome Chapel of Bones

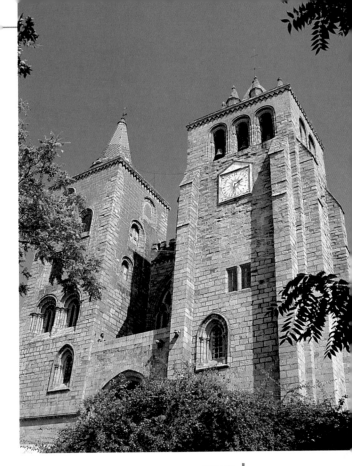

SÉ (CATHEDRAL)

⭐⭐⭐

Cross to the opposite side of the square, beyond the Roman temple, to appreciate the full glory of the 12th- and 13th-century façade, and the two huge, dissimilar towers built 400 years later. On the way in, do not miss the carved stone statues of the 12 apostles guarding the entrance. In the soaring nave, vast chandeliers hang from the vaulted ceiling.

A staircase at the back leads to the cathedral's Museum of Sacred Art, which houses a glittering collection of treasures including crucifixes and offertory chalices in gold and silver, the vestments and mitres of full episcopal pomp and ceremony and – by far the most beautiful exhibit in the museum – a 13th-century carved ivory statue of the Virgin of Paradise.

The 14th-century Gothic cloisters are reached through a door in the cathedral nave. Climb any of the corner staircases up onto the battlements for wonderful views over the town, and the plains of the Alentejo beyond.

69C2

Largo Marquês de Marialva

266 20910

Church always open; museum Tue–Sun 9–12:30, 2–5. Closed public holidays

Few

Church free; museum cheap

Above: *Évora's Cathedral, one of the wonders which make the city a World Heritage Site*

71

Évora Walk

Distance
2km

Time
3–4 hours

Start point
Largo Marquês de Marialva
➕ 69B2

End point
Praça do Giraldo
➕ 69B2

Lunch
Café Arcada (€)
📍 Praça do Giraldo
☎ 266 741777

Start outside the Convento dos Lóios (➤ 68) on the Largo Marquês de Marialva square, at the centre of which is a Roman temple.

The remains of this temple, built in the second century AD, constitute the most outstanding Roman monument in Portugal. Parts of it have been dismantled for other building works over the centuries, but six of the Corinthian-style columns on marble plinths are perfectly intact. It is particularly beautiful floodlit at night.

Before leaving the square, also check out the cathedral and municipal museum (➤ 69, 71). Walk under an arch behind the cathedral apse, and turn left to follow down a narrow street to the Antiga Universidade (Old University).

Walk around the cool, two-storey cloister and admire the fine *azulejo* tiles in the lecture rooms.

Walk down narrow Rua Conde da Serra da Tourega, turning left into Largo das Portas de Moura, where there is a fine, Manueline stone fountain, shaped as a globe. Notice the splendidly ornate façade of Casa Cordovil. Walk back across the square to Igreja da Misericórdia.

Above: *Now under protection, Évora's unique Temple of Diana was previously used as a market place*

Misericórdia is worth seeing for the fine baroque altar, and *azulejo*-embellished walls.

Return to Largo das Portas de Moura, this time turning right on to Rua Miguel Bombarda and left onto Rua da República, down to Igreja São Francisco (➤ 70). Walk back up Rua da República, and left up the hill into Praça Do Giraldo.

Opposite: *the Convento da nossa Senhora de Conceiçao in Beja, scene of a passionate love affair*

72

Évora's main square, Praça do Giraldo, is cobbled with black and white *paralelo* stones, and arcaded round the sides, leaving open-air cafés coolly shaded.

What to See in the Alentejo

BEJA ✪✪

Reputedly the hottest place in Portugal, but a pleasant town with several points of historical interest. The 15th-century **Convento da Nossa Senhora de Conceição** (on Largo Nossa Senhora de Conceiçao) is one of the most beautiful buildings in the Alentejo. It was here that the convent's most famous resident, Sister Mariana Alcoforado, had a love affair with a French count in the 17th century. Her piously erotic letters were later published as *Letters of a Portuguese Nun*.

➕ 74B2
✉ 60km south of Évora
ℹ Tourist Office: 25 Rua do Capitão J F de Sousa (☎ 284 311913)

Convento
🕐 Tue–Sun 9:45–12:30, 2–5:15
💷 Cheap

ESTREMOZ ✪✪

Ancient, fortified Estremoz, rising out of the Alentejo flatness, has a medieval atmosphere, felt particularly by those who stay in the 13th-century royal castle which dominates the town, and which has been turned into a most extraordinary *pousada*.

But just as important a part of Estremoz's fascination is to be discovered as you wander along the historic streets, many of them cobbled, between Moorish squares and past imposing façades. Rising above the royal palace section of the castle is the greyish marble Torre das Três Coroas (Tower of the Three Crowns), so-called because kings Sancho II, Afonso III and Dinis all contributed to its construction. The climb up a steep, worn staircase to the top of the keep is rewarded by a 360-degree panorama as far as Évora, and across to Spain in the east, if the weather is clear.

Within the keep is the beautiful **Capela Rainha Santa Isabel**, adorned with *azulejo* tile paintings recounting the life of this 14th-century queen and saint who dedicated her life to the poor, often in defiance of her husband King Dinis. She died in the town in 1336.

The castle is always open and the chapel opens 9:30–11:30, 2:30–5.

➕ 74C3
✉ 44km northeast of Évora
ℹ Tourist Office: Rossio do Marquês de Pombal (☎ 268 333541)

Castle keep and chapel
♿ None 💷 Moderate; chapel free

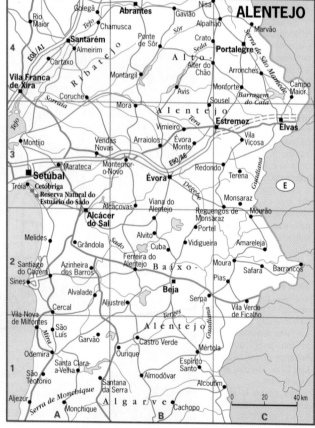

Eastern Alentejo Drive

A scenically spectacular alternative to the busy main roads between Évora and the Algarve is to take the remote, back roads near the Spanish border.

Turn off the main IP2 at Beja, taking the 260 eastwards to Serpa.

Serpa is a fine place to stop and feel the soul of the Alentejo. The old quarter is dwarfed by the rambling ruins of a fortress and old city walls. But the real joy of the town is to wander the ancient streets lined with whitewashed houses, which more than anywhere evoke the spirit of the Moors.

Take the 260 road eastwards out of town. After just 2½km, pull over at the pousada *on the right, and ask at reception for the key to the Capela São Gens.*

This simple chapel, with its plain columns inside, is believed to be one of only two original Moorish mosques surviving intact in Portugal. It is worth enjoying the hushed atmosphere of its cool interior for a few moments. Then, if it is lunchtime, try the *pousada* for good Alentejo cuisine.

Continue on the 260, then bear right on to the 265, crossing the open plains towards the ridge of mountains to the east. The country becomes increasingly wild and remote-feeling, as the road becomes twistier, and you approach Mértola.

Spectacularly perched on a narrow gorge, Mértola is at the River Guadiana's highest navigable point. Curiously, in the village is Portugal's other mosque – now the Igreja Matriz.

Meander on down the Guadiana valley on the 122 road, until you cross into the Algarve shortly past the village of Espírito Santo, and head for the resorts of the south coast.

Distance
260km

Time
5–8 hours, depending on stops

Start point
Évora
➕ 28B2

End point
Faro, Algarve
➕ 28B1

Lunch
Pousada São Gens (€€€)
(just outside Serpa, on 260 road)
☎ 284 540420

Above: *Mertola's cobbled streets are deserted during hot, summer siesta-time*

Left: *cork oaks in the Alentejo*

75

Food & Drink

A traditional Portuguese meal is a big, lusty affair involving several courses.

There are many regional variations and specialities. However, there is one food in particular which unites the national palate – *bacalhau*, or dried, salted cod. There are many different ways of preparing it, such as *Gomes de Sá* (in layers with diced potatoes, onions, olives and hard-boiled egg); and *conde de guarda* (creamed with mash and cabbage).

Many Portuguese meals begin with a bowl of steaming soup. One to look out for is *caldo verde* – cabbage shredded finely and flavoured with garlic sausage.

Fish and seafood are also much favoured and abundantly available, particularly in coastal towns. *Camarões* (shrimps), *gambas* (prawns), *sapateiro* (giant, hairy crab) and *lagosta* (lobster), all caught in the cold, deep Atlantic, are wonderful and very pricey. Among the best fresh fish are *espada* (scabbard fish), *carapau* (horse mackerel), *linguado* (sole), and of course the ubiquitous *sardinhas* (sardines). *Pescada* (hake) can be good, too, but make sure it is *fresca* (fresh) not *congelada* (frozen).

Sardines can be sizzling on the charcoal barbecue within minutes of landing on Portimão's quayside

The meat dishes in Portugal may be presented as a casserole or grilled on a skewer, be it *bife* (steak), *porco* (pork), *frango* (chicken) or *cabrito* (kid). In the north, stew is often cooked and served in an earthenware pot called a *pucara*. *Frango na pucara*, for example, is a chicken casserole. In the south, particularly the Alentejo, the hinged, metal *cataplana*, which snaps shut like a clam and sizzles with anything the cook has decided to put in, is widely seen. Sometimes, meat and fish appear in the same dish, for example in dishes such as *cataplana alentejana*, which has both shellfish and pork in it. This is a particularly delicious combination.

Wines and Port

Port is Portugal's most famous liquid export. In Vila Nova de Gaia, opposite Porto, it is available for tasting free of charge in the many shippers' houses (▶ 26).

In general, Portuguese table wines emulate the food in being good, honest, characterful and unencumbered by

too much subtlety or finesse. Internationally, the best known Portuguese wine is *Mateus Rosé*, which was invented in the 1950s for the export market.

Among the light whites, dry, slightly sparkling *vinho verde* from the Minho is a favourite all over the country and goes particularly well with fish and seafood. Other good whites to look out for include wines from *Dão* and *Serradayres*. In the Algarve the very cheap local wines from *Lagoa* are good, but they don't travel well.

For reds, the big, gutsy wines from *Dão* and *Bairrada* in the Beiras are found all over the country and are good accompaniments to the wholesome country fare. A couple of more esoteric reds to look out for include *Tinto da Anfora* and the excellent though expensive *Quinta da Bacaloa* made from French Cabernet Sauvignon grapes.

Dried fruit set out for sale at Nazaré, on the Beiras coast

Enjoying the café life in Sines, birthplace of Vasco da Gama

74C3
📧 42km east of Estremoz and 10km from the Spanish border
ℹ️ Tourist Office: Praça da República next to the main bus stop (☎ 268 622236)

Above: *Marvão Castle, a key defensive post to keep an eye on Spain*

74C4
📧 24km north of Portalegre
ℹ️ Tourist Office: Rua Dr Matos Magalães (☎ 245 993886)

ELVAS ⭐⭐

Elvas stands on the Portuguese border with Spain and its character has always been shaped by its strategic position. The formidable old town sits within great sturdy ramparts – entrance can only be achieved by passing through the old stone gateways. The walls are far more than a gesture of defiance, during the 17th century the ramparts withstood years of repeated and sustained assault and sieges. During the Peninsular War in 1801 Elvas again withstood Spanish attacks and it was despite, rather than because of this that Portugal was forced to capitulate to Spain after the Spanish declared war over Portugal's refusal to break the ancient Anglo-Portuguese alliance. Ten years later, it was from Elvas Wellington launched his siege of Badajos.

That Elvas's old quarter is very much lived-in is evident from the sheets flapping from washing lines slung between buildings, from the urchins who make the ancient squares their playground, and from the hooting of a delivery van as it tries to negotiate an alleyway constructed a thousand years ago for pedestrians and donkeys. Since the opening up of Portugal's border with Spain, Elvas has thrived from the traffic flowing between the two Iberian capitals, providing cheap eateries and lodgings close to the main N4 road.

MARVÃO ⭐⭐⭐

This small and remote medieval town, perched high on a peak of the São Mamede ridge, which forms a natural border with Spain, has inspired poets such as José Amaro, who wrote of Marvão that 'You have Portugal at your feet and, in opening your arms, Spain'. For centuries its dramatic location, encased by sheer cliffs, was the reason for its existence and survival as it was virtually unassailable.

A tortuous road now leads up to the craggy summit, where a *pousada* has been built among the handful of tightly clustered houses within the walls, which can be walked round for stupendous views over to Spain.

MONSARAZ (➤ 20, TOP TEN)

VILA VIÇOSA   ✪✪

This royal city was once the seat of the Dukes of Braganza, the family which provided Portugal with its monarchs from 1640 until the proclamation of the Republic in 1910. It is worth stopping at, to visit the **Paço Ducal (Ducal Palace)**, whose 110m-long marble façade forms one side of the main square.

The palace is now a museum, filled with huge paintings depicting Portugal's military triumphs – particularly those over the Spanish – along with displays of fine art, porcelain, tapestries and other treasures from the royal era. Also worth seeing are a collection of royal carriages and the kitchens, where enormous, gleaming copper cauldrons and huge roasting spits evoke the era of royal hunting and feasting.

✚ 74C3
✉ 18km southeast of Estremoz
ℹ Tourist Office: Praça da República (☎ 068 881170)

Paço Ducal
☎ 068 98659
🕐 Apr–Sep daily 9:30–1, 2:30–5:30 (Sat–Sun until 6); Oct–Mar Tue–Sun 9:30–1, 2–5. Closed public holidays
✋ Expensive

Vila Viçosa

The Algarve

When Portuguese from elsewhere in the country say *Algarve não é Portugal* – 'The Algarve is not Portugal' – they are referring to several factors which separate this province from the rest of the country. The main difference is the strong Moorish influence to the culture; architecture, food, place-names, words in local dialects and even the physical appearance of some Algarvians.

The other main difference is the Mediterranean-type climate which the Algarve enjoys. This, of course, is what has been responsible for the explosion in tourism, turning an agricultural and fishing-based economy into one dependent on holiday-makers from northern Europe, in a single generation.

---

*'...the Algarve... is not
Andalusia's far west,
but Portugal's deep south.
It should be visited first by
the foreigner who has
already been in Portugal
for several months.'*

HENRY MYHILL,
British traveller
(1969)

Left: *Praia da Rocha*

Faro

Faro is the capital of the Algarve, whose airport, just west of the city, is the main gateway for the several million tourists who visit the south coast resorts every year. It is built at the edge of a wide lagoon surrounded by wetlands and salt flats, 10km from a vast beach splintered into sandy islands, some of which emerge and disappear with the tide.

Faro was an important Moorish city which was captured by Afonso III in the dying days of Arab rule in Portugal. It continued to flourish until 1596 when, under Spanish occupation, the town was sacked and burnt by the British. In 1755 it was again destroyed – this time by the great earthquake, more famous for having reduced Lisbon to rubble. But despite this, an attractive walled old town and a few historic monuments survive, warranting an incursion into the heart of the city.

Faro Cathedral, whose side chapels are adorned with 17th- and 18th-century tiles

What to See in Faro

CAPELA DOS OSSOS (CHAPEL OF BONES) ✪✪
Like its better-known counterpart in Évora, the walls of this small, ghoulish ossuary in the crypt of the Igreja do Carmo are lined with human bones and the grinning skulls of long-deceased monks, reminding visitors of the certainty of their death.

✚ 89D1
✉ Largo do Carmo
🕐 Mon–Fri 10–1, 3–5/6, Sat 10–1
♿ None
📖 Moderate

MUSEU MARÍTIMO (MARITIME MUSEUM) ✪
This museum, housed in the harbour master's office on the seafront, is dedicated to the industry on which Faro's prosperity has depended for centuries – fishing. Models of numerous vessels demonstrate the evolution of the fishing boats and have been recreated with infinite care and detail. Rooms full of other fishing equipment are also on display, including crab and cuttlefish traps and harpoons for spearing shark and tuna.

✚ 89D1
✉ Rua Comunidade Lusiada
☎ 289 803601
🕐 Mon–Fri 2:30–4:30. Closed public holidays
♿ Few
📖 Moderate

SÉ (CATHEDRAL) ✪✪
A jumbled mixture of Gothic, Renaissance and baroque of no great architectural distinction. However, the 17th- and 18th-century *azulejos* in the side chapels on both sides of the nave are worth seeing. The darkened interior can also be deliciously cool on a hot day.

✚ 89D1
✉ Largo da Sé
🕐 Mon–Fri 10–1, 2–5. Sat and Sun, open only during services
ℹ️ Tourist Office: Rua da Misericórdia (☎ 289 803604)
♿ Few
📖 Cheap

Did you know ?

Faro was sacked and burnt by the Earl of Essex in 1596. Although England and Portugal were allies at the time, this was the period of annexation by Spain, with whom Britain was at war.

Above: *chapel in the grounds of Igreja do Carmo, better known for its Chapel of Bones*

Faro Walk

Distance
3km

Time
2–4 hours, depending on stops

Start point
Jardim Manuel Bivar
✚ 89D1

End point
Museu Marítimo
✚ 89D1

Lunch
Dois Irmãos (€€€)
✉ Largo Terreiro do Bispo
☎ 289 823337

Storks alight on the highest points they can find, such as the belfry of Faro's Igreja do Carmo

Start at Jardim Manuel Bivar

These well-tended gardens look out across the harbour and are the only part of town where there is some sense of peace and open space as seabirds call and halyards clink on masts.

From the south end of the gardens, enter the old town through the stone arch next to the Turismo. This is the 18th-century Arco da Vila, with its statue of Thomas Aquinas. A short walk along the Rua do Municipo leads into the Largo da Sé (Cathedral Square) and the Sé itself (➤ 83).

Cross the Praça Afonso and leave the old town through the Arco de Repousa, turning left into Rua Manuel Francisco, then right at the crossroads into Rua Santo António main shopping street and just before at the Praça da Liberdade, onto Rua de Portugal. Adjacent to the end of this road is a white-fronted building housing the Teatro Lethes.

Inside the former Jesuit college of Santiago Maior, now the Teatro Lethes, is a chapel converted into a tiny replica of La Scala, Milan's famous opera house. The building stages varied art and other exhibitions.

Cross the Largo das Mouras Velhas and turn right up Rua do Sol, then left, crossing Rua do Alportel into Largo do Poço, which leads into Largo do Carmo.

In the middle of Largo do Carmo stands the Igreja do Carmo, a Carmelite church, whose alluring, if macabre, feature is the Capela dos Ossos (➤ 83).

Return to the Largo do Poço, and follow the Rua Alistão Vardim as far as Rua 1 de Maio. Turn right here, rejoining the harbour at Praça Francisco Gomes, at the north end of Jardim Manuel Bivar. Walk round the north of the harbour, ending at the Museu Marítimo (➤ 83).

What to See in the Algarve

ALBUFEIRA ✪

Albufeira has become a symbol of the transformation, within a single generation, of the Algarve's fishing communities into a string of metropolises catering for huge numbers of sun-seeking tourists from northern Europe.

However, Albufeira still retains some of its original quaint charm. There are cobbled streets and whitewashed cottages squatting at the feet of apartment blocks; hidden away, there are two simple, rather lovely, old churches – Capela de Misericórdia (Chapel of Mercy) and the Igreja de São Sebastião (Church of Saint Sebastian); down on the beach there are still fishermen who draw their gaily-painted wooden boats up onto the sand and sell their catches by Dutch auction.

CABO DE SÃO VICENTE (► 18–19, TOP TEN)

LAGOS ✪✪✪

History-packed Lagos is among the most attractive of the Algarve's coastal towns. To a large extent it has survived the advent of tourism with its charm intact, because most of the development has been outside the town.

In Praça Infante Dom Henrique there is a large bronze statue of Henry the Navigator holding his sextant and gazing out to sea. Leading off from the square are cobbled, pedestrianised streets lined with cafés, bars and restaurants where you can sit and eat or drink *al fresco* while enjoying the cheerful ambience.

88C2
39km west of Faro
Tourist Office: Rua 5 de Outubro (☎ 289 585279)

Above: *Albufeira is the ultimate fishing village turned mega-resort*

88B2
16km west of Portimão
Tourist Office: Largo Rua Vasco da Gama (☎ 282 763031)

MONCHIQUE

88B3

Monchique is 25km north of Portimão

Tourist Office: Largo dos Chorões (☎ 282 911189)

The best day to visit the main town of the Monchique hills is the second Friday of every month, when there is a large market with farmers from a wide area bringing their produce for sale, as well as ceramics and handicrafts.

Foia, the highest peak in the Algarve (902m), overlooks the town, offering the most sensational views on a clear day. Four kilometres south of Monchique are the Caldas de Monchique, a therapeutic spa since Roman times. Enjoy walks in the countryside around the 19th- and 20th-century complex, which boasts state of the art treatments.

PORTIMÃO

88B2

62km west of Faro

Tourist Office: Avenida Zeca Afonso (☎ 282 470732) and Avenida Tomás Cabreira, Praia de Rocha (☎ 282 419132)

Portimão is surrounded by an ugly urban sprawl, though there are a few points of interest for those who penetrate the centre, such as the Largo Primero de Dezembro, and the fine Igreja Matriz. There is also excellent shopping on the cobbled walkways between Rua do Comércio and Rua Vasco da Gama.

Seafood is landed fresh each morning at the town quayside and the simple seafood restaurants just off the dock are some of the most atmospheric places on the Algarve to enjoy charcoal grilled sardines.

Opposite: *nature has sculpted extraordinary forms on Praia da Rocha*

Below: *fresh sardines with salad and bread are irresistible to holidaymaking diners*

Portimão's beach is at Praia da Rocha (2km from town), which, in the early days of the Algarve's tourism, was the jewel of the coast, magnificently overhung by red sandstone cliffs and pitted with numerous caves. The huge beach of fine sand is strewn with rugged outcrops sculpted by nature into weird formations and backed now by huge hotel complexes.

SAGRES ✪✪✪

The small town where Prince Henry the Navigator set up his famous School of Navigation is out on the very corner of Europe. The scenery is suitably dramatic: solid, bare, windswept bluffs with steps hewn out of them lead down to beaches (not illustrated) where the tide washes round in great sweeps, while gulls swirl and hover high above.

✚ 88A1
✉ 33km west of Lagos
ℹ Tourist Office: Rua Comandante Matoso
(☎ 282 624873)

Western Algarve Drive

Distance
165km

Time
4–6 hours including stops

Start point
Lagos
88B2

End point
Lagos
88B2

Lunch
Praia do Castelejo
beach café (€)

Start from Lagos. Take the 125 westwards, signposted Sagres (▶ 87). Continue 6km along the cliff-top road, to Cabo de São Vicente (▶ 18–19). Return to the road junction just above Sagres, and take the 268 northwards, signposted to Vila do Bispo. Go into the village and take the narrow road behind the town stadium signposted Prai do Casteljo.

The huge beach of Praia do Castelejo is backed by high cliffs and gets few visitors. The sea is rough and often cold, tempting only a few dedicated surfers. However, it is an excellent place to appreciate the raw beauty of the western Algarve, and to lunch in the beach café.

Return to Vila do Bispo, and continue north on the 268 to Aljezur.

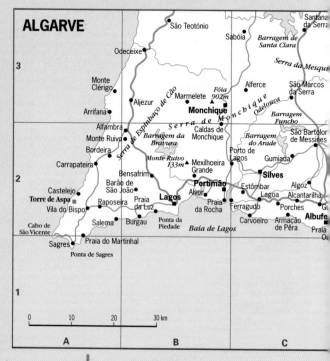

Elsewhere in Europe, the old town of Aljezur, topped by a ruined castle, might have a turnstile, official guide and ice-cream stall. But climb to the castle for wonderful views over the west coast, and you will probably have the place to yourself.

From Aljezur, take the 267 inland (eastwards), into the gentle green Monchique hills, to the town of Monchique (➤ 86). Four kilometres south of Monchique, just off the 268, is the pretty spa town of Caldas de Monchique.

Caldas de Monchique is where the ubiquitous Monchique mineral water comes from. On the main square are some fine old façades belonging to the era of 19th-century gentility when the spa was popular with wealthy Spaniards. Some delightful trails lead off into the woods, from just behind the square.

The 268 continues south, through orchards and citrus groves, rejoining the 125 west of Portimão. Turn right to return to Lagos.

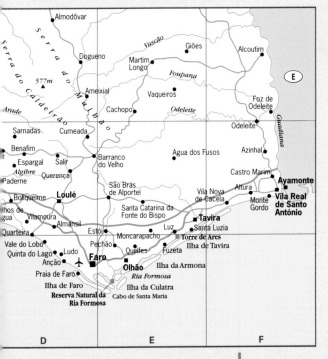

🕂 88C2

✉ 7km northeast of Portimão

ℹ Tourist Office: Rua 25 de Abril (☎ 282 442255)

Museum of Archaeology

✉ Rua das Portas de Loulé

☎ 282 444832

🕐 Mon–Sat 9–6

▨ Moderate

🕂 89D1

✉ 15km west of Faro

🕂 89D2

✉ 26km west of Faro

Above: *tourists peruse the local lace in Silves, the ancient Moorish capital of the Algarve*

SILVES ✪✪✪

Silves was the old Moorish capital of the Algarve, recaptured by Christian forces in 1249. It was an Atlantic port until the River Arade, on which it stands, silted up. The aura of the Moors lives on, as you will discover if you take a walk round the old, restored castle walls. Also worth seeing is the 13th-century Sé de Santa Maria (Cathedral), and the **Museum of Archaeology**, which puts the town's history into context.

TAVIRA (► 25, TOP TEN)

VALE DO LOBO ✪✪

A modern, up-market, purpose-built tourist complex of over 750 luxury villas, swimming pools, restaurants, boutiques, nightclubs, tennis courts (including the famous David Lloyd Tennis Centre), next to some of the Algarve's finest golf courses. It is all very beautifully done in typical low, domed, whitewashed Algarvian architectural style. The resort has everything except local culture and a beach; for these, residents have to leave the complex gates and brave the real world.

VILAMOURA ✪✪

The most extensive tourist complex in Portugal. Vilamoura started off as a development of posh villas around a superb golf course; now there are four 18-hole courses and a wide range of villas, apartments and hotels. Vilamoura has neither the exclusive air of Vale de Lobo nor the seediness of Albufeira, although elements of each can be found in the sharply contrasting 'villages' which make up the giant resort. The sports facilities are the best in the Algarve; as well as the golf courses, there are more than 50 tennis courts and all kinds of watersports around a huge marina with over 1,000 berths.

Where To...

Above: *willow baskets heaped in the sun in Monchique*
Right: *statue of São Vicente*

The North

Prices

Approximate prices for a three-course meal for one person are shown by € symbol:

€ = under €15
€€ = €15–€30
€€€ = over €30

Amarante

Adega Regional Kilowatt (€)
Artisan produced air-dried ham in country bread accompanied by glasses of *vinho verde* is all this tiny rustic eatery serves. The perfect lunch!

✉ **Rua 31 de Janeiro** ☎ **255 433159** 🕐 **Closed evenings and Sun–Mon**

Zé da Calçada (€€€)
Some think this restaurant overpriced for good though not outstanding food. But the view over the stone bridge and town are superlative and a treat to savour.

✉ **Rua 31 de Janeiro**
☎ **255 422023**

Barcelos

Casa dos Arcos (€€)
Good homey cooking with excellent bread and fish. Don't even think of coming without making a reservation if it is a Thursday (that is, market day).

✉ **Rua Duques de Bragança**
☎ **253 811975** 🕐 **Closed Mon**

Braga

A Toca (€)
Highly recommended for a lunchtime snack if you are sightseeing in the town. Sandwiches, savoury and sweet pastries, plus a *prato do dia* (dish of the day) are all served here.

✉ **127 Rua do Souto**
☎ **253 623279**

Pousada de Amares (€€€)
The exceptional vaulted stone dining room makes an atmospheric place to eat excellent regional Minho cuisine.

✉ **Amares (north of Braga)**
☎ **253 371971**

Bragança

Lá em Casa (€€)
Best place in town to eat. *Lá em casa* means 'at home'. Bearing this in mind, the fish and meat dishes are surprisingly elaborate.

✉ **Rua Marques de Pombal**
☎ **273 322111**

Restaurante Poças (€)
This bustling restaurant over two floors is popular with locals. Located in the *residencial* of the same name.

✉ **Rua Combatentes da Grande Guerra** ☎ **273 331428**

Coimbra

Cozinha (€€)
Cosy, exceptionally friendly and family-run. Homey Portuguese cooking including top-notch *bacalhau Gomes de Sá* (sliced and served with potatoes and hard boiled eggs).

✉ **Rua Azeiteiras 65**
🕐 **Closed Mon**

Zé Manel (€€)
The atmosphre is jaunty and studenty during the academic term, and the restaurant remains popular, though more sedately so, during vacation time. The *cabrito* (kid) is excellent.

✉ **12 Beco do Forno**
☎ **239 823790**

Guimarães

Vira Bar/Restaurant (€€–€€€)
This modern wine bar/restaurant set in a historic town house has a relaxing

ambiance. Portuguese and international dishes.

✉ **Largo Condessa do Juncal**
🕐 **Closed Sun and Mon**

Porto

Café Majestic (€)

A wonderful 18th-century gilt and mirrored city centre café. Perfect for a snack lunch.

✉ **Rua da Santa Catarina 112**
☎ **22 200 3887**

Filha da Mãe Preta (€€)

Richly atmospheric and mildly raunchy restaurant on the quayside. If you are brave enought to risk trying *tripas à Portuguesa* (tripe with beans), this is the best place to do it.

✉ **Cais da Ribeira 39**
☎ **22 205 5515**

Ora Viva (€€)

Bijou restaurant one street back from the riverside. The menu concentrates on seafood.

✉ **Rua Fonte Taurina 83**
☎ **22 205 2033** 🕐 **Closed Sun and Mon**

Portucale (€€€)

Superb views can be enjoyed from the penthouse plus top-notch international cuisine and modern interpretations of traditional dishes.

✉ **598 Rua da Alegria**
☎ **22 570717**

Postigo do Carvão (€€)

Traditional *bacalhau* and seafood with rice are specialities here along with other Portuguese dishes. There's regular live music.

✉ **Rua Fonte Taurina**
☎ **22 200 4539** 🕐 **Closed lunch and Mon**

Restaurante Chinês (€€€)

Superb Cantonese food is served in this authentic restaurant run by immigrants from Portugal's colony of Macau. Just on the Porto side of the Dom Luis I bridge's upper level, there are great views across to Vila Nova de Gaia.

✉ **Avenida Vimara Peres 38**
☎ **22 200 8915**

Sabadores d'aleia (€)

Small café-snack bar located on the river-front where the Portuguese workers, rather than tourists, choose to eat and drink.

✉ **Avenue Ramos Pinto, Vila Nova de Gaia** 🕐 **Closed Sun in winter**

Taverna dos Bebóbos (€€)

Traditional Porto and Minho fare down on the quayside. A long established restaurant, but now very popular with tourists.

✉ **Cais da Ribeira 24**
☎ **22 313565**

Valença do Minho

Pousada de São Teotónio (€€€)

For your first or last meal in Portugal coming from, or *en route* to, Spain, have it here with views across the Minho. Excellent regional cuisine.

☎ **251 824020**

Vila Real

Espadeiro (€€)

Vila Real's top restaurant, which serves excellent *bacalhau*, trout and suckling pig. There is also an extensive wine list.

✉ **Avenida Almeida Lucena**
☎ **259 322302**

Tripas

Porto's most famous regional dish, *tripas à Portuguesa* (tripe with beans) is not for the squeamish. It could be said that this plateful of white, leathery internal organ is to *nouvelle cuisine* what Vasco da Gama was to ballet dancing.

Lisbon & Central Portugal

Bread

The universal staple in Portugal is the crusty roll known as a *pãozinho* in the north, and a *papo seco* in Lisbon and the south. The coarse and heavy but characterful *broa* is made from maize, rye or corn meal.

Alcobaça

Trindade (€€)
Right by the abbey and an excellent place to round off a sightseeing session.
🖂 22 Praça Dom Henriques
☎ 262 842397 🕔 Closed Sat

Batalha

Pousada do Mestre Afonso Domingues (€€€)
The *pousada*, right next to the monastery, serves a fine meal, preceded by delicious cured ham and cheesy titbits.
☎ 244 896260

Cascais

Casa Velha (€€€)
Elegant dining amid a rather exclusive clientele. This is a very popular restaurant so booking is essential.
🖂 Avenida Bomval 1 ☎ 21 483 2586

Chequers (€€)
English pub serving a range of beers plus English and Portuguese food. Lots of tables out in sunny Luis de Camões square make for a 'beer garden' atmosphere.
🖂 Largo Luís de Camões 7
☎ 21 483 0926

Jardim dos Frangos (€)
Grilled chicken and sardines with fresh salad form the main menu items at this exceptional budget restaurant. Expect to queue but it's worth it.
🖂 Avenida Marginal ☎ 21 486 1717 🕔 Closed Mon Oct–Apr

O Pescador (€€€)
Renowned fish restaurant with celebrity and royal clientele. Excellent choice of fresh seafood but the paella is a speciality.
🖂 Rua das Flores 10B ☎ 21 483 2054

Leiria

Restaurante Jardim (€€)
Good regional food, which includes grilled trout, served in view of both the river and the castle.
🖂 Jardim Luis de Camões

Lisbon

Belcanto (€€€)
Formal restaurant serving classic Portuguese cuisine including locally renowned *Ovos à Professor*, an egg dish.
🖂 Largo de São Carlos
☎ 21 342 0607 🕔 Closed Sun

Bota Alta (€)
A small, simple restaurant at the heart of the Bairro Alto serving good, hearty food.
🖂 Travessa da Queimada 34–7
☎ 21 342 7959

Forno Velho (€€)
A first rate Brazilian restaurant serving large plates of barbecued meats and *feijoada* (bean stew).
🖂 Rua do Salitre 42, Avenida da Liberdade

Gambrinus (€€€€)
Best place in the Baixa district for seafood and fresh fish.
🖂 Rua Portas de Santo Antão 25 ☎ 21 342 1466

São Jerónimo (€€)
Excellent modern restaurant with a good range of soups and seafood close to the attractions of western Lisbon.

loyal Portuguese clientele.
🖂 **Rua dos Jerónimos 12**
☎ **21 364879** ⓘ **Closed Sat and Sun**

Sua Exelencia (€€€)
Romantic little restaurant in the Lapa district, where the owner often introduces himself personally to the guests.
🖂 **40–2 Rua do Conde**
☎ **21 390 3614** ⓘ **Closed Wed**

Tágide (€€€)
One of Lisbon's top restaurants, located on fashionable Rua Garrett. High class international cuisine.
🖂 **Largo da Académia National de Belas Artes 18** ☎ **21 342 0720** ⓘ **Closed Sun**

The Frog (€)
This is a great place to relax and have a drink and snack after your visit to the Expo-park. Lively young crowd, especially in the evenings.
🖂 **Parque de Nações**
☎ **21 895 2898** ⓘ **Open until 2AM Mon–Fri, 4AM Sat–Sun**

Óbidos

A Ilustre Casa de Ramiro (€€€)
Continental cuisine served in an atmospheric dining room of stone and deep pastel pink stucco decorated with huge terracotta amphora – a magnet for the 'smart set'.
🖂 **Rua Porto do Vale** ☎ **262 959194** ⓘ **Closed lunch and Sun in winter**

Muralhas (€€)
Fashionable and arty visitors to Óbidos come here for high quality, traditional Portuguese cooking.
🖂 **Rua Dom João de Ornelas**
☎ **262 950930**

Pousada do Castelo (€€€)
A richly atmospheric and romantic place in which to dine. It's also very popular and can get busy, so reserving a table is highly recommended.
☎ **262 955080** ⓘ **Closed Tue**

Santarém

O Mal Cozinhado (€)
Excellent value food served in this restaurant, which has a lot to live up to, as it is located in the town which holds a well-regarded annual gastronomic fair.
🖂 **Campo da Feira**
☎ **243 823584**

Setúbal

Pousada de São Filipe (€€€)
The magnificent views from the terrace atop the fortress walls matches the food served at this most dramatic *pousada*.
🖂 **Fortress São Filipe**
☎ **265 550070**

Sintra

Cantinho de São Pedro (€€€)
Top quality French and Portuguese cuisine served at a restaurant with high standards, and prices to match.
🖂 **18 Praça Dom Fernando II**
☎ **21 923 0267** ⓘ **Closed Mon and Wed evening**

Tacho Real (€€)
This restaurant serves a selection of excellent food, both Portuguese and international, at reasonable prices.
🖂 **Rua da Ferreira 4**
☎ **21 923 5277** ⓘ **Closed Mon**

Nibbles
Saucers of locally cured meats, cheese, almonds, olives and other titbits frequently arrive, unsolicited, on restaurant tables. These are not generally 'free' – you pay as you pick, with prices shown on the menu. Sometimes, however, particularly in *pousadas*, they are included in the *table d'hôte* prices. To clarify matters, point to them and ask if they are *'incluido?'*

Alentejo

Pork and Clams

Porco à Alentejana, a speciality of the region, is one of Portugal's most interesting dishes, consisting of pork stewed with clams. One theory is that the dish originated in the 15th-century when Jews were expelled from Portugal or forced to convert to Christianity. They were served this dish to test whether they had really severed links with the old faith.

Beja

Alentejano (€€)
Real, as opposed to designer-tourist Alentejo food is served here. Locals favour the brimming bowls of soup and big hunks of pork.
✉ 6–7 Largo dos Duques de Beja ☎ 284 323849

Churrasqueira o Alemão (€)
Good choice of barbequed meats at this smarter than average *churrasqueira*.
✉ Largo des Duques ☎ 284 311490

Crato

Pousada Flor da Rosa (€€€)
Stunning contemporary dining room in the modern extension to this historic *pousada* serving local and international dishes.
✉ 730 Crato ☎ 245 997210

Elvas

Canal 7 (€)
The best of a large number of cheap restaurants, conveniently located where much international road traffic stops to eat.
✉ Rua dos Sapateiros 16 ☎ 268 623593

Centro Artistica Elvense (€)
An excellent place for a quick, tasty snack or the more substantial dish of the day. Next to the bus station.
✉ Praça da Republica ☎ 266 703057

O Aqueduto (€€)
Excellent fish – which is unusual for a Portuguese restaurant set so far inland.
✉ Avenida da Piedade ☎ 268 623676

Estremoz

Aguias d'Ouro (€€)
Wholesome, homey local fare at reasonable prices.
✉ Praça Rossio 27 ☎ 268 337030

Pousada da Rainha Santa Isabel (€€€)
High class Alentejan food with superb views from the dining room at one of Portugal's finest *pousadas*.
☎ 268 332075

São Rosas (€€)
Cosy restaurant in the main square of Estremoz citadel serving typical Portuguese cuisine.
✉ Largo D Dinis 11 ☎ 268 333345 ◷ Closed Sun and Mon in winter

Évora

A Muralha (€)
Good café serving excellent *pasteis de carne* (meat pastries) and other snacks.
✉ Rua 5 de Outubro 21 ☎ 266 722284

Café Arcada (€)
Large art deco café on the main square in town where you can enjoy Portuguese patisserie and coffee with the locals.
✉ Praça Giraldo ☎ 268 980742

Cozinha de Santo Humberto (€€€)
The finest food you'll find in Évora. Very attentive service and excellent wine list. It's certainly expensive, but well worth it.
✉ Rua da Moeda 39 ☎ 266 749114

Luar de Janeiro (€€)
A small, cosy restaurant with

a formal touch.
- ✉ **Travessa de Janeiro 13**
- ☎ **266 724895**

Martinho (€€)
Trendy restaurant with arty flourishes, serving original interpretations of traditional Alentejo dishes.
- ✉ **24–5 Largo Luis de Camoes**
- ☎ **266 723057**

O Antão (€€)
Modern restaurant which also exhibits the work of local artists.
- ✉ **Rua João de Deus 5–7**
- ☎ **266 726459**

O da Boa Fé (€)
Small family run establishment with tables on the church square. Good value for money Portuguese food.
- ✉ **Praça 1 de Maio 23–24**
- ☎ **266 702090** ⊙ **Closed Mon lunch and Sun**

Pousada dos Lóios (€€)
An unforgettable experience: eating in the cloisters of this fabulous, converted 15th-century monastery.
- ✉ **Largo Conde de Vila Flor**
- ☎ **266 324051**

Restaurante Típico Guiao (€€)
Very popular restaurant whose *ementa Turistica* is good value.
- ✉ **Rua da República 81**
- ☎ **266 23071**

Marvão

Pousada de Santa Maria (€€€)
This is by far the best place to eat in Marvão, if only for the quite stupendous panorama out over the Alentejo plains.

- ✉ **7 Rua 24 de Janeiro**
- ☎ **245 993201**

Monsaraz

Solar de Monsaraz (€€)
Expect a warm welcome in this friendly, family-run eatery. The food is unsophisticated, but very filling.
- ✉ **38 Rua Conde de Monsaraz**
- ☎ **266 502846**

Serpa

Alentejano (€€)
Specialities at this restaurant include rich, meaty dishes and several excellent local ewe's milk cheeses, all at reasonable prices.
- ✉ **Praça da República**
- ☎ **284 553335**

Cuiça-Filho (€)
Cheap, cheerful and very friendly, family-run restaurant.
- ✉ **Rua Portas de Beja 18**
- ☎ **284 549566**

Vila Viçosa

Framar (€)
Simple restaurant run by a friendly family. Large portions at very reasonable prices.
- ✉ **35 Praça da República**
- ☎ **268 898158**

Ouro Branco (€€)
A good selection of traditional and distinctive Alentejo dishes is on offer at this restaurant, including excellent soup.
- ✉ **Campo da Restauração**

Pousada D João IV (€€)
Quality regional food in the dining room of this former convent.
- ✉ **7160 Vila Viçosa** ☎ **268 980742**

Local Wines
The Alentejo is gradually emerging as a leading wine-growing area, for both reds and whites. Esporão, Redondo and Borba are all names to look out for.

Algarve

Menus
In certain tourist areas, the law requires restaurants to offer a three-course *menu turistica*, inclusive of drinks and coffee, at a set price. While these can be good value (particularly if you see locals tucking into them), too many places seem to have settled on a monotonous routine of vegetable soup, grilled hake (frozen) and ice cream.

Albufeira

Atrium (€€€)
Splash out for a romantic meal with a good variety of fish, international cuisine and an excellent wine list.
✉ Rua 5 de Outubro
☎ 289 515755

Tasca Viegas (€€)
The closest thing you will find in Albufeira to a typically Portuguese restaurant.
✉ Cais Herculano 2
☎ 289 514087

Almancil

Fuzio's (€€€)
A blend of Mediterranean and New World cuisine in this beautifully renovated Portuguese house.
✉ Almancil Road/Val do Lobo
☎ 289 399019 ⓘ Closed Wed

São Gabriel (€€€)
One of a few restaurants in this select area of the Algarve to have earned a Michelin star. International menu. Bookings essential.
✉ Quinto do Lago ☎ 289 394521 ⓘ Closed lunch and Mon

Burgau

Beach Bar (€)
The amalgamation of every-thing the Algarve does so well; excellent grilled sardines and other fish with a terrace on the sand of a sandy beach.
✉ Burgau (west of Lagos)
☎ 282 697553 ⓘ Closed Mon out of season

Carrapateira

Sitio do Forno (€€)
Panoramic views of Amado beach and the Atlantic from the cliff-side terrace, and excellent fresh fish.
✉ Praia do Amado ☎ 963 558404 ⓘ Closed Mon

Faro

A Tasca (€)
An excellent, very traditional tavern, of a kind that is hard to find in the Algarve.
✉ Rua do Alportel 38
☎ 289 824739

Cidade Velha (€€)
Pleasant and cosy restaurant that is well located in Faro old town. The menu offers a selection of traditional southern cuisine.
✉ Rua Domingo Guieiro 19
☎ 289 827145

Dois Irmãos (€€€)
Generally considered to be one of Faro's best haunts, serving a range of excellent fish and seafood dishes.
✉ Largo Terreiro do Bispo 20
☎ 289 823337

Mesa dos Mouros (€€)
Pretty converted house in the cathedral square with a small terrace and cosy dining room.
✉ Largo de Sé ☎ 289 878873
ⓘ Closed Mon lunch and Sun

Muralhas de Faro (€€€)
This beautifully styled restaurant set in the old city walls serves Alentejo and Moroccan dishes. Lovely dining room and very nice terrace.
✉ 1–7 Rue e Beco do Repuso
☎ 289 824839

Lagos

Dom Sebastião (€€€)
A very popular, top-notch restaurant, serving a wide range of international and

southern Portuguese dishes. Be sure to book ahead, especially in summer.
🖂 20–2 Rua 25 de Abril
☎ 282 762795

Millenium Jardin (€€)
Situated in an open terrace and mezzanine, the international menu has a range of fresh fish on ice.
🖂 78 Rua 25 de Abril
☎ 282 762897

Piri-Piri (€€)
Unsurprisingly, the speciality here is hot, spicy chicken *piri-piri*. It goes well with cold beer.
🖂 Rua Alfonso d'Almeida 10

Monchique

Restaurant Bica-Boca (€€)
One of Western Algarve's best restaurants with a menu of Portuguese and international dishes. Just north of town on the Lisbon road.
🖂 Estrada de Lisboa
☎ 282 912271

1692 (€€€)
The terrace of this up-market restaurant within the renovated spa complex is the perfect place for a long lunch or romantic dinner. Mainly international menu.
🖂 Caldas de Monchique
☎ 282 910910

Praia de Luz
Fortaleza da Luz (€€)
The remains of the town's 16th-century fortress now plays host to a restaurant serving Portuguese dishes and fresh fish. Nice terrace and garden.
🖂 3 Rua de Ingreja ☎ 282 789926 🕓 Closed mid-Nov to mid-Dec

Sagres

A Tasca (€€)
Fresh fish and enchanting views of the harbour.
🖂 At the port ☎ 282 464177

O Telheira do Infante (€€–€€€)
Good options of snack bar or full service restaurant (concentrating on seafood dishes). Large terrace overlooking the beach.
🖂 Praia de Mareta
☎ 282 624179

Pousada do Infante (€€€)
You need time for a long, leisurely lunch or dinner here. Excellent food and cliff top location.
☎ 282 464222

Silves

Café Ingles (€)
Elegant 1920s mansion with a large terrace under the shadow of Silves cathedral. Good range of Portuguese and international snacks.
🖂 11 Escalada do Castello
☎ 282 442585 🕓 Closed Sat Oct–Apr

Tavira

Imperial (€€)
Well known for its big, fresh, meaty fish steaks.
🖂 Rua José Pires Padinha 22
☎ 281 322306 🕓 Closed Wed

O Cantinho das Espetadas (€€)
Traditional Portuguese restaurant with regional specialities. One of only a few places in the Algarve that hosts *fado* (Saturday PM)
🖂 22 Rua Dr Augusto da Silva Carvalho ☎ 918 801292
🕓 Closed Sun

Snacks
Cafés are an excellent bet for cheap snack lunches. Nationwide standard fare includes *rissois de camarão* (shrimp rissoles), *bolinhos de bacalhau* (deep fried cod balls), *pregos* (steak sandwiches) and a panoply of sweet and gooey wonders.

The North

Prices
Approximate prices per room per night, regardless of double or single occupancy
€   = under €70
€€   = €70–€120
€€€   = over €120

Alijó

Pousada de Barão Forrester (€€€)
Superb *pousada*, recently given a face lift. Surrounded by port vineyards.
✉ Rua José Rufino
☎ 259 959215

Amarante

Hotel Navarras (€€)
A good and comfortable hotel, convenient for all the town's major sights.
✉ Rua Murtas-Madelena
☎ 255 422106

Amares

Pousada Santa Maria do Bouro (€€€)
This converted Cistercian Monastery is one of the most historic Portuguese *pousadas*. The austere architectural lines have been matched with elegant décor, especially in the vast stone dining room.
✉ 4720–688 Amares
☎ 235 371971

Arcos de Valdevez

Casa da Ponte (€€)
Late 17th-century country mansion next to the River Vez offering the perfect quiet retreat for walking and boat trips and is ideally placed for touring the far north.
✉ Rua dos Milagres 78
☎ 0258 516107;
www.casadaponte.net

Barcelos

Quinta do Convento da Franqueira (€€)
A beautiful Turismo de Habitacão in a sea of *vinho verde* vineyards, next to a ruined monastery about 5km from Barcelos. The English owners rent just three rooms. Booking essential.
✉ Pereira ☎ 253 831606

Braga

Hotel de Parque (€€)
A fine old hotel that has recently been renovated. Friendly and comfortable.
✉ Parque de Bom Jesus do Monte ☎ 253 676548

Hotel Residencial D Sofia (€)
Refurbished hotel set on a quiet square in the city. Reasonable sized rooms make a good budget base.
✉ Largo de S João do Souto 131 ☎ 253 263160

Bragança

Pousada de São Bartolomeu (€€€)
This modern *pousada*, which has the added advantage of wonderful views over the castle and town, offers good quality accommodation with an on site restaurant.
✉ Estrada do Turismo, 5300–271 Bragança
☎ 273 331493;

Coimbra

Bragança (€€)
A wonderfully located hotel that is packed with good, old-fashioned charm.
✉ Largo das Ameias 10
☎ 239 822171

Quinta das Lágrimas (€€€)
Travellers who want to get away from the hustle and bustle can enjoy a relaxed stay in this peaceful, characterful old house.
✉ Santa Clara ☎ 239 802 380;
www.quintadaslagrimas.com

Gêres

Pousada São Bento (€€€)
The beautiful location of this mountain chalet amid a forested national park offers superb views and excellent hiking from the door.
✉ 4850–047 Caniçada
☎ 253 649150

Guimarães

Pousada de Santa Marinha da Costa (€€€)
A richly atmospheric *pousada* in a converted monastery.
☎ 253 511249

Mesão Frio

Pousada Solar de Rede (€€€)
Perfect location for touring the Douro Valley, this fine restored 18th-century mansion is set in large manicured gardens.
✉ Santa Christina
☎ 254 890130

Porto

Albergaria Miradouro (€€)
A comfortable, friendly place in the same building as the penthouse Portucale restaurant, one of Porto's best.
✉ Rua da Alegria 598
☎ 22 530717

Boa Vista (€€)
This is Porto's *only* hotel with a sea view. Small and charming, though out of the way at Foz do Douro.
✉ Esplanada do Castelo 58
☎ 22 532 0020;
www.hotelboavista.com

Infante de Sagres (€€€)
Porto's only grand, sumptuous, old-style hotel. Antique-stuffed rooms and immaculate service.
✉ Praça Dona Filipa de Lencastre 62 ☎ 22 339 8500;
www.hotelinfantesagres.pt

Malaposta (€€)
In a convenient location, Malaposta offers a smart modern interior.
✉ Rua da Conceição 80
☎ 22 200 6278;
www.hotelmalaposta.com

Pestana Porto (€€€)
Located on the Praça de Ribeira overlooking the river and quayside at Vila Gaia, on the doorstep of the best bars and restaurants in town.
✉ Praça de Ribeira 1 ☎ 22 340 2300; www.pestana.com

Viana do Castelo

Pousada do Monte de Santa Luzia (€€€)
Famous old hotel, now a *pousada*. Amazing views over the Minho coast.
✉ Monte de Santa Luzia
☎ 258 828889

Valença do Minho

Pousada de São Teotónio (€€€)
Peaceful location with views over the Mihno river, this *pousada* sits inside the walls of the old fort.
✉ 4930–619 Valença do Minho
☎ 251 800260

Vila Nova de Cerveira

Pousada Dom Dinis (€€€)
This beautiful 13th-century manor house is one of Portugal's smaller *pousadas*. It is unique because each room has its own courtyard.
✉ 4920–296 Vila Nova de Cerveira ☎ 251 708120

Turismo de Habitacão
This is a nationwide scheme designed to accommodate tourists in private houses in rural Portugal. Typically this will be an old country house with just two or three guest rooms, usually with private bathrooms. Breakfast is included but whether dinner is provided is up to the hosts. Often if guests want an evening meal they simply join the family table.

Lisbon & Central Portugal

York House
York House in Lisbon is so called because in the last century it belonged to two ladies from Yorkshire in northern England. Despite this, it is as Portuguese as can be, bedecked with *azulejo* tiles and full of Portuguese antique furniture.

Alcobaça

Hotel Santa Maria (€)
This modest, friendly hotel is the best of a very limited choice of lodgings in town.
✉ Rua Dr Francisco Zagalo
☎ 262 597395

Batalha

Residencial Casa do Outeiro (€)
This modern small pension makes a good budget option. All rooms have terraces, some with views of the monastery. Small pool.
✉ Largo Carvalho do Outeiro 4
☎ 244 765 806;
www.casadoouteiro.com

Cascais

Hotel Albatroz (€€€)
A superb, if very pricey, luxury hotel in a converted palace. The old rooms have more character but a new wing offers greater comfort.
✉ Rua Federico Arouca
☎ 21 484 7380

Vila Galé Village (€€€)
Large resort hotel set in verdant gardens close to Cascais marina with facilities such as sauna and choice of swimming pools.
✉ Rua Frei Nicolau de Oliveira, Parque de Gandarinha ☎ 21 482 6000; www.vilagale.pt

Estoril

Hotel Palácio do Estoril (€€€)
The old-fashioned, though stylish, hotel where the crowned heads of Europe have hob-nobbed over the decades.
✉ Rua do Park ☎ 21 464 8000; www.hotel-estoril-palacio.pt

São Cristovão (€€)
Beautiful, very small seafront *pensão* that has managed to retain its character.
✉ Avenida Marginal
☎ 21 468 0913

Fátima

Best Western Dom Gonçalo (€€)
Refurbished modern hotel set in woodland. A popular spot with pilgrims.
✉ Rua Jacinta Marto 100
☎ 249 539330; www. estalgemdomgoncalo.com

Hotel de Fátima (€€)
Although a touch lacking in character, this hotel is the largest and most comfortable place to stay in Fátima.
✉ Rua João Paulo II
☎ 249 532351

Lisbon

Alegria (€)
Very friendly, fairly basic *pensão* located in the Baixa.
✉ Praça da Alegria 12
☎ 21 347 5522

As Janelas Verdes (€€)
Restored 18th-century mansion house in the Lapa district. There is a small garden with a terrace where you can relax.
✉ Rua das Janelas Verdes 47
☎ 21 396 8143; www.heritage.pt

Avenida Palace (€€€)
Classical, old-style opulence and superlative service.
✉ Rua 1 Dezembro 123
☎ 21 321 8180; www.hotel-avenida-palace.pt

Hotel da Lapa (€€)
A sybaritic hotel, each room individually styled, in the quiet Lapa district.

✉ Rua do Pau da Bandeira 4
☎ 21 394 9494; www.lapa-palace.com

Hotel Lisboa Plaza (€€)
A very good standard hotel, centrally located.
✉ Travessa do Salitre 7 ☎ 21 321 8218; www.heritage.pt

Internacional (€€)
Very comfortable and reasonably priced, though lacking in character.
✉ Rua da Betesga 3
☎ 21 324 0990; www.hotel-internacional.com

Roma (€)
Pleasant little *pensão*, near the Avenida da Liberdade.
✉ Travessa da Gloria 22a
☎ 21 346 0057

Solar do Castelo (€€)
A medieval structure close to Castelo São Jorge tastefully converted into a stylish hotel.
✉ Rua das Cozinhas 2 ☎ 21 231 8200; www.heritage.pt

Tivoli Lisboa (€€€)
A famous hotel, offering elegance and sophistication.
✉ Avenida da Liberdade 185
☎ 21 319 8900;
www.tivolihotels.com

York House (€€€)
Converted monastery offering the atmosphere of a country *quinta*.
✉ Rua das Janelas Verdes 32
☎ 21 396 2435;
www.yorkhouselisboa.com

Óbidos

Albergaria Rainha Santa Isabel (€€)
A modest friendly place with rooms with balconies overlooking a narrow street.
✉ Rua Direita ☎ 262 959323

Estalagem do Convento (€€)
A former convent immediately outside the main gate into the walled town.
✉ Rua João de Ornelas
☎ 262 959217; www.estalgemdoconvento.com

Pousada do Castelo (€€€)
Portugal's smallest *pousada*, and one of the most romantic places in the country to stay.
☎ 262 955080

Palmela

Pousada de Palmela (€€€)
Glorious *pousada* within ancient stone walls. Superb views over the Arrábida peninsula.
✉ Castelo de Palmela 2950
☎ 21 235 1226

Queluz

Pousada da Dona Maria I (€€€)
A wonderful *pousada*, and convenient for visiting the Peninsular War battle sites.
✉ Largo Palácio de Queluz
☎ 21 435 6158

Sintra

Palácio de Seteais (€€€)
A converted 18th-century palace of overwhelming grandeur, set in spectacular gardens.
✉ Rua B du Bocage 8
☎ 21 923 3200

Tomar

Estalagem Santa Iria (€€)
Enchanting little inn on an island. Convenient for the town sites and for river walks.
✉ Parque do Mouchão
☎ 249 313 326

Pousadas
Pousadas are state-run inns and hotels, which make up an excellent network of accommodation outside the cities. Several are national monuments; others are modern, but built at historic sites. A third category are modern lodges built in locations chosen for their wild remoteness and wonderful views. For further information about most of the *pousadas* listed here see www.pousadas.pt

Alentejo

Lusitanos
Several fine, thoroughbred *Lusitano* horses are stabled at the Horta de Moura hotel in Monsaraz. They can be ridden across the Alentejo plain from here. *Lusitanos* were originally bred for bullfighting, and are today most famous for dressage.

Beja

Pousada de São Francisco (€€€)
Splendidly converted, 13th-century monastery.
✉ **Largo Dom N Alvares Pereira** ☎ **284 328441**

Residencial Bejense (€)
This prettily decorated town house in the centre of town is an excellent budget option.
✉ **Rua Capitão Francisco de Sousa 57** ☎ **284 311570**

Residencial Cristina (€€)
Modern, friendly, good value hotel, conveniently located.
✉ **Rua de Mertola 71** ☎ **284 323035**

Crato

Pousada Flor da Rosa (€€€)
A Templar castle, convent and palace are brought together with an ultra-modern extension to create a picturesque *pousada*.
✉ **7430–999 Crato** ☎ **245 997210**

Elvas

Pousada de Santa Luzia (€€€)
A comfortable, modern *pousada* outside the walls. Good restaurant serving traditional local specialities.
✉ **Avenida de Badajoz** ☎ **268 622194**

Quinta de Santo António (€€€)
Exquisite old inn, luxuriously restored.
✉ **São Bras** ☎ **268 628406**

Estremoz

Páteo dos Solares (€€€)
Historic *quinta* now transformed into a luxury hotel. Some rooms have a fireplace or Jacuzzi.
✉ **Rua Brito Capelo** ☎ **268 338400**

Pousada da Rainha Santa Isabel (€€€)
A touch austere perhaps, but this is the closest most people in the modern world get to the atmosphere of a medieval castle.
✉ **Largo Dom Dinis** ☎ **268 332075**

Évora

Pousada dos Lóios (€€€)
Another atmospheric *pousada* where you can sleep in the monastic cells and dine in the cloisters.
✉ **Largo do Conde de Vila Flor** ☎ **266 724051**

Residencial Diana (€)
This small cosy hotel in the heart of the town is within a couple of minutes walk from the Cathedral and Praça do Giraldo.
✉ **Rua Diogo Cão 2–3** ☎ **266 702 008**

Marvão

Pousada de Santa Maria (€€€)
Quite simply one of the most sensationally located *pousadas* in Portugal: hence the high prices.
✉ **Rua 24 de Janeiro** ☎ **245 993201**

Vila Viçosa

Pousada D João IV (€€€)
This former convent makes the ideal luxurious base for touring the eastern Alentejo.
✉ **7160 Vila Viçosa** ☎ **268 980742**

Algarve

Albufeira

Sheraton Algarve (€€€)
A complete resort (also known as Pinecliffs) with golf course, spa, watersports and other attractions.
⊠ Praia de Felésia (east of Albufeira) ☎ 289 5000100; www.pinecliffs.com

Faro

Hotel Eva (€€€)
Faro's top hotel with spacious rooms overlooking the harbour and sea.
⊠ Avenida da Republica ☎ 289 803354

Lagos

Caza de São Gonçalo (€)
Atmospheric old town house in the heart of Lagos where rooms are decorated in Portuguese style with period furniture. Garden and terrace.
⊠ Rua Cândido dos Reis ☎ 282 762171

Loulé

Loulé Jardim (€)
A small, peaceful hotel. A particularly good place to feel the traditional spirit of the Algarve.
⊠ Praça Manuel de Arriaga ☎ 289 413094

Monchique

Termas de Monchique (€–€€)
A range of accommodation at the thermal spa ranging from self-catering apartments to a pension or inn. Spa treatments charged separately.
⊠ Caldas de Monchique ☎ 22 910910; www.monchiquetermas.com

Portimão

Penina (€€€)
A very famous golf hotel: this is where the Beatles stayed during the 1960s. It now belongs the Meridien group.
⊠ PO Box 146 – between Portimão and Lagos ☎ 282 420200

Praia da Rocha

Hotel Oriental (€€€)
This luxurious beautifully designed small hotel, with its distinctive oriental touches, sits overlooking the beach at Praia da Rocha.
⊠ Avenida Tomás Cabreira ☎ 282 480800; www.tdhotels.pt

Sagres

Pousada do Infante (€€€)
With its quite sensational location on the bluffs of Sagres, this *pousada* is set in one of the wildest spots of the Algarve.
⊠ Ponta de Sagres ☎ 282 464222

Silves

Hotel Colina dos Mouros (€)
Modern Moorish-style hotel across the valley with views of Silves. Good value for the facilities on offer.
⊠ 8301 Silves ☎ 282 440420

Tavira

Vila Galé Albacora (€€€)
Beautiful low-level hacienda-style hotel located on the river 3km outside Tavira. An excellent place to relax, with pools, spa and gym.
⊠ Quatro Águas ☎ 281 380800; www.vilagale.pt

Azulejos
Glazed, hand-painted tiles, or *azulejos*, are found all over Portugal, particularly in the south. This art form – usually, though not always in blue – is a direct legacy of the Moors. *Azulejos* decorate churches, railway stations and ordinary homes. The best *azulejo* souvenirs are square-shaped paintings on panels of 16 or 25 tiles.

Shopping in Portugal

Pottery

Traditional Portuguese pottery starts at a base level with the ubiquitous cockerels of Barcelos and bawdy creations found in rural markets. Better value is the *barro* glazed earthenware crockery available all over the country. At the top end of the market is the internationally famous *Vista Alegre* porcelain, still much cheaper in Portugal than in the many countries to which it is exported.

Handicrafts and Souvenirs

Barcelos

Tourist Office

Excellent selection of local handicrafts and pottery, including the famed Barcelos cockerels.

⊠ **Largo da Porto Nova**

Évora

A Casa

One of a plethora of handicraft shops along this arterial street.

⊠ **Rua 5 de Outubro 57A**

Alforge

Small but high quality collection of handicrafts, wine and foodstuffs.

⊠ **Rua da Alcarcova de Biaxi 1**

Coisas do Monte

Excellent collection of woven woollen shawls, scarves and blankets, plus other local handicrafts.

⊠ **Rua de Manços 16**

Lisbon

Centro de Turismo e Artesanato

A wide range of ceramics, glass, leather and other handicrafts, from all over Portugal. Packing and shipment can be arranged.

⊠ **Rua Castillo 61B**

Loulé

Bicas Velhas

Excellent for simple pottery. Watch the potters at work at their wheels.

⊠ **Rua das Bicas Velhas**

Monchique

Casa dos Arcos

Monchique's speciality is simple, folding wooden chairs. They are easily transportable and this is the place to buy some of the best.

⊠ **Rua Auguste Gulbenkian**

Óbidos

A Artesã

Comprehensive collection of Portuguese linen and cotton tablecloths, napkins etc. from mass produced to expensive hand woven and embroidered.

⊠ **Rua Direita 91**

Solão d'Avó

Fine selection of bed throws, rugs, woollen ponchos and cork items.

⊠ **Rua Direita 40**

Portimão

Arraiolas

Arraiolas rugs from the Algarve, and many other examples of woven handicrafts.

⊠ **Rua Teofilo Braga**

Bazar-Miriamis

A great range of handicrafts and ceramics of all kinds, from the Algarve and elsewhere in Portugal. Shipment of goods can be arranged.

⊠ **Largo do Dique 11**

Porto

Ribeira Craft Centre

Very touristy but a comprehensive selection of artefacts from rugs to ceramics, mainly from the Minho and elsewhere in the north.

⊠ **Rua da Reboleira 37**

Praia da Rocha

Cerâmica

This tiny converted fisherman's cottage is filled with ceramics.

⊠ **Avenida Tomas Cabreira**

Sagres

A Mó
Large selection of traditional Algarve pottery and souvenirs.
📧 **Located on the Cabo San Vicente road**

Serpa

Tourist Office
Good selection of local handicrafts, pottery and embroidery.
📧 **Largo D João de Melo**

Sintra

Alfazema
It's hard to choose just one item from Alfazema's excellent range of fine linens and embroidery.
📧 **Largo 1 de Dezembro 10, São Pedro de Sintra**

Tavira

Portas do Castelo
Excellent range of modern cork products plus other quality *artesanato*.
📧 **1´-3 Praça da República**

Jewellery

Évora

Miranda Ferrão
Local gold and silver work including examples of filigree work.
📧 **Rua 5 Outubro 28–9**

Lagos

Triarte
Fine designer jewellery available in non-precious and precious metals. They will undertake bespoke projects.
📧 **Rua da Vedoria**

Lisbon

Casa Batalha
A long established jewellers' shop, which offers a surprisingly modern selection of jewellery, as well as their more traditional repertoire of goods.
📧 **Rua Augusta 222 and Amoreiras shopping centre**

W A Sarmento
This is one of Lisbon's longest established goldsmiths, offering a beautiful selection of jewellery. The firm can also prepare work to individual commission.
📧 **Rua do Ouro 251**

Porto

Josephus
Beautiful displays of high quality gold and silver filigree, both traditional and modern. Also a good selection of semi-precious stones. Conveniently and centrally located near the Bolhão covered market.
📧 **Rua Formosa 344**

Tavira

Stárte
This rather small jewellers' outlet offers a good quality and unusual selection in the more inexpensive sector of the market.
📧 **Rua Guilherme Gomes Fernandes 26**

Glass, Porcelain and High Quality Ceramics

Albufeira

Galeria Labisa
A range of modern styles of china, glass and pewter.
📧 **16 Avenida da Liberdade**

Lisbon

Atlantis
A full range of Atlantis crystal.
📧 **Amoreiras Shopping Centre, Avenida Duarte Pacheco**

Baskets
Portuguese woven baskets are worth bringing home. In the north they are known as *seiras* and are made from rushes dyed bright colours. Algarvian baskets are often woven from palm fronds.

Bawdy Pots

The widespread availability of pornographic pottery may shock the more prudish. However, it does allows you to glimpse the earthy side of Portuguese humour. Don't believe any earnest nonsense about 'fertility symbols'. The truth is, it's just plain bawdy!

Fábrica Ceramica Viúva Lamego

Hand-painted tiles straight from this factory that also has a shop. Some good deals on seconds.

✉ **Largo do Intendente**

Fábrica de Loiça de Sacavem

Tile paintings and other hand-painted ceramics.

✉ **Avenida da Liberdade 49–57**

Vista Alegre

Vast selection of the famous Vista Alegre tableware.

✉ **Largo do Chiado 18**

Marinha Grande
Jasmin

Hand-made high quality glass items are sold in the factory shop.

✉ **Estrada de Leiria 227**

Porches
Casa Algarve

One of the best of many local ceramics shops along this stretch of road, with an endless array of artefacts.

✉ **On the north side of the main N125**

Porches Pottery

The Algarve's most famous ceramics centre, which features many *avante-garde* creations, as well as traditional Algarvian pottery. There is also a selection of cork work.

✉ **On the south side of the N125**

Portimão
O Aquario

A very smart shop selling a selection of Atlantis crystal glass, Vista Alegre porcelain and other high quality products.

✉ **Rua Vasco da Gama**

Porto
Vista Alegre

The famous porcelain manufacturer's main outlet in the city.

✉ **Rua Candido dos Reis**

Porto de Mós
Painéis de Azulejos João Faustino

Exceptional quality panels of *azulejos* in traditional style and pattern.

✉ **Cumeira de Cima, Juncal**

Silves
Estudio Destra

Ceramic artist Kate Swift produces an excellent range of *azulejos* in modern styles and also undertakes commissions.

✉ **Largo Jeronimo Osorio**

Sintra
Cerâmicas de São Pedro

Hand-crafted *azulejos* panels. Shipping can be arranged.

✉ **Calçada de São Pedro**

Antiques

Beja
Antiquidades

A range of antiques are for sale in this shop on Beja's main square.

✉ **Largo Dom Dinis 7**

Lagos
Casa da Papagaio

Large, rambling selection of bric-à-brac, which is sure to delight the dedicated browser.

✉ **Rua 25 Abril**

Velharias

You will discover all sorts in this shop from antiques and bric-a-brac to stone troughs, brassware and ceramics.

✉ **On the N125 between Lagos and Figueira**

Lisbon
Fundacão Ricardo do Espirito Santo
Massive selection of high-class reproduction furniture, silverware, tiles and Arraiolas rugs. Shipment can be arranged.
🖂 **Largo das Portas do Sol, 2**

Portimão
A Tralha
Assorted antiques, plus a selection of Madeira embroideries.
🖂 **Rua Vasco da Gama**

Casa da Papagaio
A smaller version of its sister-shop in Lagos.
🖂 **Rua Santa Isabel**

Porto
Reis Filhos
Very smart, expensive city-centre shop selling antique furniture, leather and modern tableware.
🖂 **Rua da Santa Catarina**

Vilamoura
Secilo XIX
This small shop is situated in the marina and sells excellent china and other small items.
🖂 **Vilamoura Marina**

Wine

Faro
Pousada Porto
Reputed to be the best wine shop in Faro, including an excellent selection of Alentejo wines.
🖂 **Rua do Bocage 50**

Lisbon
Solar do Vinho do Porto
The place to buy port in the capital.
🖂 **45 Rua São Pedro de Alcântara**

Porto
Solar do Vinho do Porto
If you haven't stocked up on port over the bridge in the lodges of Vila Nova de Gaia, here's another chance.
🖂 **Quinta da Maceirinha, Rua de Entre Quintas 220**

Markets

Barcelos
One of the largest and most famous markets in Portugal.
🕐 **Thu**

Espinho
A large market selling handicrafts, ceramics, clothes and food.
🖂 **19 km south of Porto**
🕐 **Mon**

Lisbon
Flea Market
The capital's largest outdoor market for handicrafts, clothes, food, rugs and much more. Behind São Vincente church.
🖂 **Campo de Santa Clara**
🕐 **Tue, Sat**

Monchique
Farmers from a wide area bring their produce here, as well as ceramics and handicrafts aimed principally at tourists from the coastal resorts.
🖂 **Third Fri of every month**

Ponte de Lima
A colourful market in the Minho.
🖂 **Second Mon of every month**

Porto
Bolhão Market
Colourful, covered market selling food and handicrafts.
🖂 **Corner of Rua Formosa and Rua da Sá de Bandeira**
🕐 **Mon–Fri**

Medronho
A bottle of *medronho*, available in wine shops, is guaranteed to bring memories of Portugal flooding. This colourless, burning firewater is distilled from arbutus, a little berry rather like a wild strawberry.

Children's Attractions

Children First

Many visitors to Portugal, particularly those from northern European countries, are surprised by the way children are treated and catered for here. The big difference in Portugal, however, is the way children are indulged – some would say over-indulged. Elderly and young, men and women all make a tremendous fuss over children and make allowances for their needs in hotels, restaurants, shops or museums.

Entertaining children in Portugal tends to be a less formal and more pragmatic business – a question of attitude, rather than of provision of specific facilities.

On a superficial level, children's facilities are fairly minimal. There are few theme parks, zoos or other traditional forms of juvenile entertainment. There are, however, plenty of fun fairs to be found throughout the summer months: the Feira Popular in Lisbon; the Feira do Porto at the Palacio Cristal and countless motley collections of ageing dodgems, ferris wheels and candy-floss stalls at *festas* all over the country.

The great majority of children's entertainment in Portugal is located in the Algarve region.

Boat Trips and Watersports

The Algarve has some excellent child-friendly water activities whether they want to simply watch the world go by, or take part in a range of activities.

Portimão
Pirate Ship Adventure Cruise

Cave exploration, sailing or beach BBQ are three activities you can enjoy from this fully rigged caravel sailing ship.
✉ **Rua Vasco do Gama**
☎ 967 023840

Vilamoura
Polvo

Company with several boats from luxury motor yatchs,

dolphin spotting trips or small boat charter.
✉ **Vilamoura Marina**
☎ 289 301884

Silves
Silves Waterski Centre

Jetski, kneeboarding rings, banana and boat charters on the freshwater reservoir above Silves.
✉ **Barragem de Silves**
☎ 964 465614

Miscellaneous

Albufeira
Zebra Safari

Take to the back roads of the Algarve in an organised Jeep safari; morning or full-day trip.
✉ **The Strip, Montechorro**
☎ 289 583300

Almancil
Carting Almancil

Karting track inaugurated by the late Ayrton Senna; a miniature version of the Brazilian F1 track.
✉ **Sitio de Pereiras**
☎ 289 399899

Évora
Lucena Karting

Go-karts and cross-country quad adventures – great for older children.
✉ **Quinta da Lucena**
☎ 266 737700

Lisbon
Feira Popular de Lisboa

Fun fair open afternoon and evening throughout summer.
✉ **Avenida da República**
☎ 21 793 4593

Theme Parks

Alcoutim
Parque Mineiro Cova dos Mouros

This open-air museum

recreates the lifestyle of the Chalcolithic people who mined the site here 5,000 years ago. Also, the rare Iberian monkey is bred here.

✉ **10km south of Martinlongo**
☎ **281 489505**

Water Parks

In recent years, aquatic parks have enjoyed an explosion in popularity along the Algarve coast. A multitude of them has now been developed, lining the N125 main highway, most of them located between Faro and Portimão.

Albufeira
Zoomarine
This aqua park features various different marine shows, including the ever-popular performing dolphins.

✉ **N 125 Guia** ☎ **289 560300**

Lagoa
Slide and Splash
A huge complex of water chutes, slides and swimming pools to keep even the most reluctant of water-babies amused.

✉ **N125, Vale Judeu, Estombar**
☎ **282 341685**

Atlântico Park
Another complex of rides and entertainments that come with a guarantee that participants will get absolutely soaking wet.

✉ **N125, Quatro Estradas – at the crossroads with the road into Quarteira** ☎ **289 397282**

Quarteira
AquaShow
Combined waterpark and bird garden with a wax museum.

✉ **On the N396 just outside town** ☎ **289 389396**

Silves
The Big One
Another huge water park, The Big One is fully equipped with a variety of rides, tunnels and wave machines.

✉ **N125, Alcantarilha**
☎ **282 322827**

Zoos

Albufeira
Krazy World-Algarve Zoo
A real mixture of things to do from swimming pools to petting zoo to exotic animal shows to a fairground.

✉ **Signposted from the N125, Guia** ☎ **21 726 9349**

Lagos
Lagos Zoological Park
The 3ha of land here have been transformed into various habitats for monkeys, wallabies and a range of exotic birds. There is also a petting area with goats, ducks and chickens.

✉ **Barão São João, north of Lagos** ☎ **282 688236**

Lisbon
Jardim Zoológico
Not the most exciting of zoos, but the best Portugal can offer.

✉ **Estrada de Benfica 158**
☎ **21 726 9349**

Monchique
Omega Parque Jardim Zoológico
This new animal park is dedicated to the conservation and breeding of endangered species. Twenty-five different species are on view, from cheetah to rhino.

✉ **On the N266 at Caldas de Monchique** ☎ **282 911327**

Break the Ice
To travel with youngsters can be an excellent way to break the ice with locals. Children are the object of a great deal of attention in Portugal, and are constantly admired and asked after.

Eating Out
In Portugal, children of any age are welcome pretty much anywhere their parents are, including cafés and restaurants at any time of the day or night. For example, it is not uncommon for a baby to be whisked off to the kitchen to the delight of chef and staff, while parents carry on with their meal in peace.

Discos, Nightclubs & Casinos

African Rhythms
Portugal's home-grown rock music has made few international in-roads. However, it is significantly influenced by African music, brought to Lisbon by musicians from the former colonies of Angola, Mozambique, Guinea-Bissau, São Tome and Principe, and the Cape Verde Islands. Bands include GNR and Sétima Legião.

Discos and Nightclubs

Albufeira

Kiss
Wild and popular club, always packed to the gunnels from midnight to 4AM in summer.
✉ **Motechoro**

Capitulo
Chill-out at this fashionable nightspot where you can rub shoulders with celebrities.
✉ **Ed. Borda de Agua, Praia de Oura**

Liberto's
Liberto's styles itself as an up-market disco bar.
✉ **Areias de São João, Apartado 553**

Locomia
One of the most trendy disco's around found on Santa Eulália beach.
✉ **Praia de Santa Eulália**

Cascais

Coconuts
The hottest disco on the Lisbon coast, full of energetic Lisboetas and foreign tourists.
✉ **Hotel Nau, Rua Dra Irancy Doyle**

In
Club concentrating on mainstream sounds.
✉ **Cascais Casino**

Coimbra

Scotch Club
Long established club in this buzzing university city.
✉ **Quinta da Insua, Santa Clara**

Via Latina
A noisy nightclub which plays techno music.
✉ **Rua Almeida Garrett 1**

Vinyl
Latest avant-garde sounds
✉ **Avenida Afonso Henriques**

Elvas

Decibel
The prime disco-club of a range in this border town.
✉ **Praçeta dos Descombrimetos**

Leiria

Triplex Club
Very modern club/bar and restaurant for the smart set.
✉ **Avenida D João**

Lisbon

Absoluto
Disco and occasional live bands.
✉ **Rua Dom Luis 1**

Ad-Lib
Caters to a mainly 30s and 40s age group.
✉ **Rua Barata Salguiera**

Kapital
Ultra-trendy, somewhat cliquey. Mainly techno music downstairs, more middle-of-the-road on the other two floors.
✉ **Avenida 24 de Junho 68**

Kremlin
The latest of late-night venues attracting the fashionable young things of the city.
✉ **Escadinhas da Praia 5**

Lux–Frágil
A long-established but still very popular nightclub set in the heart of the Bairo Alto.
✉ **Rua da Atalaia 126–8**

Metalúrgica
A relaxed and popular

nightclub, playing a variety of music.

⊠ **Avenida 24 de Junho 110**

Plateau
Long established nightclub, that still has many devotees.
⊠ **Escadinhas da Praia 3–7**

Praia da Rocha

Kathedral Nightclub
Mixed music with theme nights, best during the summer.
⊠ **Avenida Tomás Cabreira**

Quarteira
Furna Nightclub
Latest sounds with a local crowd.
⊠ **Main street in old town**

Tomar
Index
Techno-club.
⊠ **Estrada do Prado**

Val do Lobo
Gecko Club
Up-market bar/club that attracts a celebrity crowd.
⊠ **Praça de Val do Lobo**

Vilamoura
Discoteca Marina Rock
Rock and pop catering to the holiday crowd.
⊠ **Vilamoura Marina**

Kadoc
Discotheque and live music venue in one. Excellent guest DJs throughout the year.
⊠ **Estrada Vilamoura Bolequeime**

Porto
Swing
Throbbing nightclub where Porto's trendiest hang out.
⊠ **Centro Comercial Brasilia, Rotunda da Boavista**
☎ **22 6090019**

Casinos
Gambling in Portugal is tightly controlled by law and restricted to adults. Formal attire is usually expected and you may also be asked to show your passport. Among the usual games you'll find roulette, baccarat, black jack and bingo. There are also plenty of 'one-armed bandit' slot machines. Most of Portugal's casinos are in the traditional holiday resorts such as Povoa de Varzim, on the Minho coast, where the Porto wealthy used to spend the summer season, and Estoril, for a long time one of Europe's most fashionable resorts. These have now been joined by the new establishments on the rapidly expanding Algarve.

The North
Casino da Póvoa
⊠ **Avenida Braga, Póvoa de Varim** ☎ **252 615151**

Casino Solverde
⊠ **85 Rua 19, Espinho**

Lisbon Coast
Casino Estoril
⊠ **Estoril** ☎ **214 667700**

The Algarve
Casino de Montegordo
⊠ **Vila Real de Santo António** ☎ **281 530800**

Casino da Rocha
⊠ **Edificio Tarik, Praia da Rocha, Portimão**
☎ **282 400200**

Casino da Vilamoura
⊠ **Vilamoura, Loule**
☎ **289 310000**

Night Owls
The Portuguese are night owls at the best of times, particularly the young. When it comes to nightclubs, many people take pride in the lateness of their arrival, which is often 2AM or later. Dawn is considered a good time to leave.

Theatre & *Fado*

Fado

Fado reached its greatest international phase during the 1950s, when the great *fadista* Amália Rodrigues toured the world and became, perhaps, the best known Portuguese of her generation.

Theatre

Lisbon

Teatro Nacional de Dona Maria II
Lisbon's principal theatre holds performances of Portuguese and foreign plays throughout the year except summer. All productions are in Portuguese.

✉ Rossio Square
☎ 21 325 0835

Teatro National de São Carlos
Stages opera and ballet productions and classical music concerts.

✉ Largo São Carlos
☎ 21 325 3000

Teatro Municipal de São Luis
Another grand, old-fashioned theatre where Portuguese and international companies perform.

✉ Rua António Maria Cardoso 40 ☎ 21 325 7650

Fado

Coimbra
Diligencia
A bar where *fado* is often performed, particularly during the summer academic term.

✉ Rua Nova 30 ☎ 239 827667

Lisbon
All *fado* houses serve food and levy a cover charge. You can also come just to drink and listen to the music. The majority of venues can be found in the Bairro Alto district, and stay open until around 3AM.

Adega Mesquita
A popular venue with locals and tourists.

✉ Rua Diário da Notícias
☎ 21 321 9280

A Severa
One of Lisbon's best known *fado* clubs, where many of Portugal's top *fadistas* perform.

✉ Rua das Gáveas, 55
☎ 21 342 8314

Clube de Fado
A smart modern interior for this *fado* club.

✉ Rua São João de Praça
☎ 21 885 2704

Senhor Vinho
Top-notch, genuine *fado* performances, at reasonable prices.

✉ Rua do Meio a Lapa 18
☎ 21 397 2681 🕐 Closed Sun

Timpanas
Well away from the city centre, but this venue is well worth seeking out if you are eager to listen to the real McCoy.

✉ Rua Gilberto 24, Alcântara
☎ 21 390 6655 🕐 Closed Wed

Porto
Mal Cozinhado
A convivial restaurant that is set on the Ribeira, and which is also Porto's top *fado* venue.

✉ Rua Outeirinho
☎ 22 208 1319

Tivira
Restaurante O Cantinho des Espetadas
Fado is not indigenous to the Algarve but this is one of the few places where you can hear it.

✉ 22 Rua Dr. Augusto de Silva Carvalho ☎ 918 801292
🕐 Sat 7PM

Cinema

Albufeira
Algarve Shopping
✉ On the N125, west of
Albufeira ☎ 289 560350

Almada
Warner Lusomundo
✉ Almada Forum
☎ 212 501833

Beja
Cineclub Melius
✉ Avenida Fialho da Almeida
☎ 284 321822

Barcelos
Cinema Avenida
✉ Campo 25 de Abril
☎ 253 813597

Cascais
Warner Lusomundo
✉ Cascais Shopping
☎ 214 600420

Coimbra
Cine-Teatro Avenida
✉ Avenida Sá da Bandeira
☎ 239 822131

Faro
Forum Algarve
✉ Forum Shopping Mall
☎ 289 887212

Lisbon
Amoreiras
✉ Avenida Duarte Pacheco
☎ 21 383 1275

Cine Bolso
✉ Rua Actor Taborda 27B
☎ 21 357 3407

Lusomundo
✉ Amoreiras Shopping
☎ 21 387 8572

São Jorge
✉ Avenida da Liberdade 175
☎ 21 310 3400

Tivoli
✉ Avenida da Liberdade 185

☎ 21 357 2025

Warner Lusomundo
✉ Avenida Vasco de Gama
☎ 218 922280

Warner Lusomundo
✉ Columbo Shopping
☎ 217 113200

Mértola
Mertola
✉ Centro Culturel
☎ no phone

Oporto
Warner Lusomundo
✉ Maia Shopping
☎ 229 773490

Warner Lusomundo
✉ Gaia Shopping
☎ 223 791705

Warner Lusomundo
✉ Norte Shopping
☎ 229 577040

Portimão
Golden City
✉ Modelo-de-Portimão
(shopping centre), Quinta da
Malata, Lote 1 ☎ 282 415272

Sintra
**Auditório Municipal de
António Silva**
✉ Shopping do Cacém
☎ 219 236101

**Auditório Municipal
Agualva-Cacém**
✉ Rua Coração de Maria 1
☎ 219 326101

Tomar
Cine-Templários
✉ Alameda 1 de Março
☎ 249 312837

Valença do Minho
Ciné Ibérica
✉ Centro Comericial Ibérica
☎ 251 822736

Film Fans
Portuguese are
enthusiastic cinema-goers.
Foreign films are often
released very soon after
first showings in their
native countries. They are
virtually always shown in
the original with
Portuguese sub-titles.

115

What's On When

All Portuguese towns have their own *festa's* (details from tourist offices), but these are Portugals's major festivals. Precise dates can vary.

February
Carnival weekend (which precedes Lent): festivities all over the country with streamers, fire-crackers, water-pistols and fancy dress. Particularly lively celebrations at Loulé in the Algarve, with processions through the streets and mock battles fought with almond blossom.

March
Holy Week: processions and festivals take place all over Portugal during the week leading up to Easter. The greatest concentration of these is in the north. On Good Friday, crowds gather to do penance in Braga, religious capital of Portugal, in preparation for the Easter celebrations.

May
Festas das Cruzes (Feast of the Crosses) in Barcelos (first weekend): 16 crosses symbolising the Passion of Christ are erected to mark a procession route carpeted with flowers.

Fátima Day (13 May): this is the anniversary of the first apparition of the Virgin Mary to three shepherd children at Fátima in 1917.

June
Festa de São Gonçalo (the Feast of Saint Gonçalo) in Amarante (first weekend of the month).

Festas dos Santos Populares (Feasts of the People's Saints) in Lisbon (12–29 Jun). June is the capital's month of merrymaking, with the greatest festivities on the feast of Santo António on 12 and 13 Jun.

Porto's greatest festival, *São João* (St John), coincides with the summer solstice. Bonfires are lit and a huge firework display is staged (last week in Jun).

June/July
International Music Festival – the largest arts festival in the Algarve with international artists performing at venues across the region.

July/August
Festas da Rainha Santa (Festivals of the Holy Queen) in Coimbra. A week of cultural events (first week of Jul).

The National Handicrafts Fair in Vila do Conde, on the Minho coast (last week of Jul/first week of Aug).

Festas da Senhora da Agonia (Feast of Our Lady of Suffering). Otherwise known as the *Viana Festa*, this is one of the greatest and most popular festivals in Portugal (Fri–Sun nearest 29 Aug).

September
The wine harvest festival at Palmela, across the Tagus from Lisbon (second Sun in Sep).

November
National Gastronomic Fair in Santarém in the Ribatejo with samples of food and wine from all the different regions of Portugal (first week in Nov).

Practical Matters

Above: *cockerels, Barcelos market*
Right: *elderly woman in traditional black*

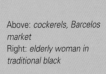

TIME DIFFERENCES

GMT
12 noon

Portugal
12 noon

→
Germany
1PM

←
USA (NY)
7AM

→
Netherlands
1PM

→
Spain
1PM

BEFORE YOU GO

WHAT YOU NEED

● Required
○ Suggested
▲ Not required

Some countries require a passport to remain valid for a minimum period (usually at least six months) beyond the date of entry – contact their consulate or embassy or your travel agency for details.

	UK	Germany	USA	Netherlands	Spain
Passport/National Identity Card	●	●	●	●	●
Visa (regulations can change – check before booking your journey)	▲	▲	▲	▲	▲
Onward or Return Ticket	▲	▲	▲	▲	▲
Health Inoculations	▲	▲	▲	▲	▲
Health Documentation (Reciprocal Agreement Document) ➤ 123, Health	●	●	▲	●	●
Travel Insurance	○	○	○	○	○
Driving Licence (national)	●	●	●	●	●
Car Insurance Certificate (if own car)	●	●	●	●	●
Car Registration Document (if own car)	●	●	●	●	●

WHEN TO GO

Portugal

High season
Low season

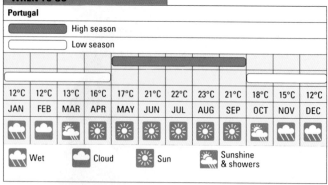

12°C	12°C	13°C	16°C	17°C	21°C	22°C	23°C	21°C	18°C	15°C	12°C
JAN	FEB	MAR	APR	MAY	JUN	JUL	AUG	SEP	OCT	NOV	DEC

🌧 Wet　　☁ Cloud　　☀ Sun　　🌦 Sunshine & showers

TOURIST OFFICES

In the UK
Portuguese National Tourist Office,
Portuguese Embassy
11 Belgrave Square,
London SW1X
☎ 0845 355 1212;
www.portugalinsite.com

In the USA
Portuguese Trade and Tourism Office,
590 Fifth Avenue,
4th Floor,
New York
NY 10036–4704
☎ 212/354 4403
Fax: 212/764 6137

POLICE 112	
AMBULANCE 112	
FIRE 112	
FOREST SAFETY 117	

WHEN YOU ARE THERE

ARRIVING

Portugal has three international airports – Lisbon, Porto and Faro. Scheduled and charter flights arrive daily at all of them from the UK and the rest of Europe, and there are direct flights to Lisbon, and charter flights to Porto, from North America.

Lisbon (Portela de Sacavem) Airport
Kilometres to city centre   **Journey times**

7 kilometres

🚆	N/A
🚌	30 minutes
🚗	15 minutes

Faro Airport
Kilometres to city centre   **Journey times**

4 kilometres

🚆	N/A
🚌	15 minutes
🚗	10 minutes

MONEY

The Portuguese unit of currency is the euro. Euro banknotes and coins were introduced in January 2002. Banknotes are in denominations of 5, 10, 20, 50, 100, 200 euros and coins are in denominations of 1, 2, 5, 10, 20 and cents, and 1 and 2 euros. Euro travellers' cheques are accepted, as are major credit cards in the large towns and cities. Credit and debit cards can be used for withdrawing euro notes from cashpoints.

TIME

 Portuguese time is the same as Greenwich Mean Time. The clocks are advanced one hour in spring, and brought back one hour in autumn. Continental Europe is always one hour ahead.

CUSTOMS

 YES
From another EU country for personal use (guidelines)
800 cigarettes, 200 cigars, 1 kilogram of tobacco
10 litres of spirits (over 22%)
20 litres of aperitifs
90 litres of wine, of which 60 litres can be sparkling wine
110 litres of beer

From a non-EU country for your personal use, the allowances are:
200 cigarettes OR
50 cigars OR 250 grams of tobacco
1 litre of spirits (over 22%)
2 litres of intermediary products (eg sherry) and sparkling wine
2 litres of still wine
50 grams of perfume
0.25 litres of eau de toilette
The value limit for goods is 175 euros

Travellers under 17 years of age are not entitled to the tobacco and alcohol allowances.

NO
Drugs, firearms, ammunition, offensive weapons, obscene material, unlicensed animals.

UK	Germany	USA	Netherlands	Spain
21 392 4000	21 881 0210	21 727 3300	21 396 1163	01 347 2381

WHEN YOU ARE THERE

TOURIST OFFICES

Visitors can call free phone 800 296 296 for information from across Portugal.

Costa de Lisboa
● Turismo de Lisboa,
Rua de Turqueira,
1300 Lisboa (Lisbon)
☎ 21 361 0350
Fax: 21 361 0359;
www.visitlisboa.com

Costa de Prata
● Região de Turismo do
Centro, Largo da
Portagem, 3000 Coimbra
☎ 239 855930
Fax: 239 825576

Costa Verde
● Comissão Municipal de
Turismo do Porto, Rua
Clube dos Fenianos 25,
4000 Oporto (Porto)
☎ 22339 3472
Fax: 22 332 3303

Montanhas
● Região de Turismo de Dão
Lafões, Avenida
Gulbenkian, 3510 Viseu
☎ 232 422014
Fax: 232 421864

Planícies
● Região de Turismo de
Évora, Rua de Aviz 90, 7000
Évora ☎ 266 742535
Fax: 266 705238

Algarve
● Região de Turismo do
Algarve, Avenida 5 de
Outubro 18, 8000 Faro
☎ 289 800400
Fax: 289 800489

NATIONAL HOLIDAYS

J	F	M	A	M	J	J	A	S	O	N	D
1	1	2	2	2	2		1		1	1	4

1 Jan	New Year's Day
Feb/Mar	Shrove Tuesday
Mar/Apr	Good Friday
25 Apr	Liberty Day
1 May	Labour Day
May/Jun	Corpus Christi
10 Jun	Portugal Day
15 Aug	Feast of the Assumption
5 Oct	Republic Day
1 Nov	All Saints' Day
1 Dec	Independence Day
8 Dec	Feast of the Immaculate Conception
25 Dec	Christmas Day

OPENING HOURS

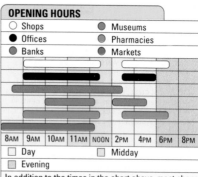

In addition to the times in the chart above, most shops close at 1PM on Saturday and are closed Sundays. In shopping centres located in cities and larger towns shops are open 10AM up to 11PM Monday to Saturday, sometimes Sunday as well. In tourist resorts and cities some supermarkets are open until 9PM. Hypermarkets are open 10AM to 11PM. As for pharmacies, each area has a pharmacy open until midnight, the location of which is advertised on pharmacy doors.
Most museums stick roughly to the opening times in the chart but many close Monday while some places also close Wednesday.

DRIVE ON THE RIGHT

TOILETS CHARGE

PUBLIC TRANSPORT

Internal Flights TAP Air Portugal ☎ 289 800200; www.tap.pt and Portugália ☎ 21 842 5559; www.pga.pt connect Lisbon, Porto and Faro. Portugália operates a *Ponte Aero* (Air Bridge) commuter service between Lisbon and Porto/Faro; no advance booking is needed, just turn up. Charter flights are also available.

Trains The national railway company, Caminhos de Ferre Portugueses (CP) ☎ 21 346 5022; www.cp.pt, runs three types of service: *Regional* (stopping at most stations); *Intercidade* (stopping at only a few large towns); and *Rapido* (express train between Lisbon and Porto). Fares are reasonable with many discount schemes.

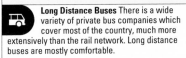
Long Distance Buses There is a wide variety of private bus companies which cover most of the country, much more extensively than the rail network. Long distance buses are mostly comfortable.

Ferries From Lisbon, ferries cross the Rio Tejo to the suburb of Cacilhas every 10 to 15 minutes (from 7AM to 9PM) from Fluvial terminal, adjacent to Praça do Comércio, or Cais de Sodré (24-hour service), taking 15 minutes. From Setúbal there is a 24-hour service across to the Tróia Peninsula, at least hourly, journey 20 minutes.

Urban Transport In the main towns there is a complete public transport network. In Lisbon the state-owned Carris company runs buses, the underground (*Metropolitano*), quaint electric trams (*eléctricos*), and funiculars and lifts (both called *elevadores*). Useful guide: *Rede de Transportes Públicos.*

CAR RENTAL

Prices are relatively cheap. You will find the major inter-national companies in Lisbon, Porto and the Algarve. If using one of the many local firms offering competitive rates, check the vehicle is in good condition and that adequate insurance is included.

TAXIS

These are cream in colour, and are good value by western European standards. In towns meters are used; it is worth checking that they are switched on. Outside urban areas the charge is per kilometre. Between 10PM and 6AM the rate increases by 20 per cent.

DRIVING

Speed limit on motorways (*autoestradas*): **120kph**; minimum: **40kph**

Speed limit on dual carriageways: **100kph**; country roads: **90kph**

Speed limits on urban roads: **50kph**

Seat Belts must be worn in front seats at all times and in rear seats where fitted.

Random breath testing. Never drive under the influence of alcohol.

Fuel (*gasolina*) is available in three grades: super (98 octane), *sem chumbo* (unleaded 95 octane), and *super sem chumbo* (unleaded 98 octane). Prices vary by a few cents around the country. Filling stations are open 8AM to midnight (some 24 hours). The carrying of petrol in cans in cars is forbidden.

Orange SOS telephones are located at regular intervals along motorways and other main roads. A breakdown service is operated by the national motoring organisation, the Automóvel Club de Portugal (ACP). For assistance from the club, ☎ 213 180 100; www.acp.pt. Place a red warning triangle 30m behind your vehicle.

CENTIMETRES

0 1 2 3 4 5 6 7 8

INCHES

0 1 2 3

PERSONAL SAFETY

Theft from cars and other petty crime is increasingly a problem, especially in the Algarve. Car stereos are particularly at risk. The Polícia de Segurança Pública are the urban police to whom any crime should be reported; in tourist areas, some wear red armbands with CD on them. Remember:

- Never leave anything of value in your car.
- Do not leave valuables on the beach or poolside.
- Leave valuables in hotel safe deposit boxes.
- Don't walk alone through dimly lit areas at night.

Police assistance:
☎ **112**
from any call box

TELEPHONES

Most public telephones now accept coins and credit cards or phone cards. Phone cards can be bought at newsagents and in bars and can be used for international calls. Most hotels will also have international direct dialling but will add a large premium to the bill. Check the hotels pricing policy before making a call.

International Dialling Codes

From Portugal to:

UK:	00 44
Germany:	00 49
USA:	00 1
Netherlands:	00 31
Spain:	00 34

POST

Post Offices
There is at least one *correio* (post office) in every town and reasonably large village. They sell stamps as do many places with *correios* signs. In small towns they close for lunch, otherwise hours are:
Open: 8:30AM–6PM
Closed: Sat and Sun

ELECTRICITY

The native power supply is: 220 volts

 Sockets take two-round-pin continental-style plugs. Visitors from the UK require an adaptor and US visitors a voltage transformer.

TIPS/GRATUITIES

Yes ✓ No ✗		
Restaurants (if service not included)	✓	10%
Cafés/bars	✓	10%
Taxis	✓	10%
Tour guides	✓	€1
Porters	✓	€1
Chambermaids	✗	
Cloakroom attendants	✓	50c
Hairdressers	✓	10%
Theatre/cinema usherettes	✗	
Toilets	✗	

PHOTOGRAPHY
What to photograph: the shimmering Costa de Prata (Silver Coast), colourful fishing ports, ancient villages, hilltop castles and the rugged mountains of the north east.
Restrictions: do not take photographs at airports, military bases, military docks or anywhere your action could be construed as breaching security.
Buying film: all popular brands and types of film and camera batteries are readily available and are reasonably priced.

HEALTH

Insurance
EU nationals receive emergency medical treatment with the relevant documentation (Form E111 for UK nationals), but medical insurance is still advised and is essential for all other visitors. US visitors should check their insurance coverage.

Dental Services
Dental treatment for EU nationals is very limited under the state scheme. You will probably have to pay and the charges are not refundable; other visitors will certainly have to pay. Private medical insurance will cover you.

Sun Advice
Sunburn and sunstroke are common problems in summer (especially during July and August), particularly in the south of the country. Do not be deceived by a cooling wind off the Atlantic. Avoid prolonged exposure and use a sunscreen or cover up.

Drugs
Prescription and non-prescription drugs and medicines are available from pharmacies (*fármacias*), distinguished by a large green cross. Pharmacists have a high degree of training and can prescribe remedies for a wide range of ailments.

Safe Water
Tap water is generally safe but not too pleasant. Anywhere, but especially outside the main cities, towns and resorts, it is advisable to drink bottled water (*água mineral*), either *sem gás* (still) or *com gás* (carbonated).

CONCESSIONS

Students/Youths The International Student Identity Card (ISIC) for students, and the International Youth Card (IYC) for those under 26, entitles holders to discounts on transport and fees for museums and attractions. The Cartão Jovem (youth card), for those between 12 and 26, gives a 50 per cent discount on rail journeys over 50km.
Senior Citizens Winter holidays in the Algarve are popular with older travellers. Low-cost, flight-only deals are available from some countries, and you can find long-term accommodation for a fraction of the high-season rate. Over 65s (on proof of age) receive a 50 per cent reduction on all suburban trains, except weekdays between 6:30–9:30AM and 5–8PM.

CLOTHING SIZES

Portugal	UK	Rest of Europe	USA		
46	36	46	36		Suits
48	38	48	38		
50	40	50	40		
52	42	52	42		
54	44	54	44		
56	46	56	46		
41	7	41	8		Shoes
42	7.5	42	8.5		
43	8.5	43	9.5		
44	9.5	44	10.5		
45	10.5	45	11.5		
46	11	46	12		
37	14.5	37	14.5		Shirts
38	15	38	15		
39/40	15.5	39/40	15.5		
41	16	41	16		
42	16.5	42	16.5		
43	17	43	17		
34	8	34	6		Dresses
36	10	36	8		
38	12	38	10		
40	14	40	12		
42	16	42	14		
44	18	44	16		
38	4.5	38	6		Shoes
38	5	38	6.5		
39	5.5	39	7		
39	6	39	7.5		
40	6.5	40	8		
41	7	41	8.5		

WHEN DEPARTING

- Remember to contact the airport on the day prior to leaving to ensure the flight details are unchanged.
- You must report to the departure terminal of the airport not later than the time indicated on your ticket and/or the published timetables.
- You must comply with the import regulations of the country you are travelling to (check before departure).

LANGUAGE

The native language is Portuguese, a Latin language like French, Italian and Spanish. A knowledge of Spanish and/or French makes Portuguese easy to read, however, speaking it is somewhat trickier. Despite obvious similarities between Spanish and Portuguese spelling, Portuguese words sound very different from their ostensible Spanish equivalents. Even so, almost all Portuguese understand Spanish and in the tourist areas English is widely spoken. However, knowing a few Portuguese words will make your trip more rewarding. Below is a list of some words that might be useful. More extensive coverage can be found in the AA's *Essential Portuguese Phrase Book* which lists over 2,000 phrases and 2,000 words.

hotel	*hotel*	breakfast	*pequeno almoço*
room	*quarto*	toilet	*banho*
...single/double	*simples/de casal*	bath	*banheira*
...one/two nights	*livre*	shower	*duche*
...per person/per room	*um/doi noite(s)* *por pessoa/por quarto*	balcony	*varanda*
		key	*chave*
		room service	*serviço de quarto*
reservation	*reserva*	chambermaid	*camareira*
rate	*preço*	television	*televisão*

bank	*banco*	American dollar	*dólare americano*
exchange office	*casa de câmbio*	exchange rate	*câmbio*
post office	*correio*	bank card	*cartão do banco*
counter	*guiché*	credit card	*cartão de crédito*
money	*dinheiro*	giro bank card	*cartão dos correios*
small change	*dinheiro trocado*	cheque	*cheque*
foreign currency	*moeda estrangeira*	traveller's cheque	*traveller cheque*
pound sterling	*libra esterlina*	giro cheque	*cheque de correio*

restaurant	*restaurante*	starter	*entrada*
bar/café	*café*	dish	*prato*
table	*mesa*	main course	*prato principal*
menu	*ementa*	dish of the day	*prato do dia*
tourist menu	*ementa turística*	dessert	*sobremesa*
wine list	*lista de vinhos*	drink	*bebida*
lunch	*almoço*	waiter	*garçom/empregado*
dinner	*jantar*	bill	*conta*

aeroplane	*avião*	bus	*autocarro*
airport	*aeroporto*	..station	*estação de camionetas*
flight	*vôo*		
train	*comboio*	..stop	*paragem de autocarro*
..station	*estação caminho de ferro*		
		ferry	*barco*
ticket	*bilhete*	..port	*estação marítima*
..single/return	*ida/ida e volta*	timetable	*horário*
..first/second class	*primeira/segunda classe*	seat	*lugar*
		non-smoking	*não funadores*

yes	*sim*	help!	*ajuda!*
no	*não*	today	*hoje*
please	*se faz favor*	tomorrow	*amanhã*
thank you	*obrigado*	yesterday	*ontem*
hello	*óla*	how much?	*quanto?*
goodbye	*adeus*	open	*aberto*
excuse me!	*desculpe!*	closed	*fechado*

INDEX

Acknowledgements
The Automobile Association wishes to thank the following libraries, photographers and associations for their assistance in the preparation of this book:

IMAGES COLOUR LIBRARY cover (c): fishing boat
MARY EVANS PICTURE LIBRARY 10a, 11, 14
MRI BANKERS' GUIDE TO FOREIGN CURRENCY 119
PICTURES COLOUR LIBRARY cover (a): Albufeira, 31
SPECTRUM COLOUR LIBRARY 47
ZEFA PICTURES LTD 26

The remaining pictures are from the Association's own library (AA PHOTO LIBRARY) and were taken by:
M BIRKETT 9b, 19, 48, 51, 63b, 73, 75, 80, 83, 86, 87, 90; J EDMANSON 8b, 25, 62, 67, 68b, 71, 74, 76, 77b, 81, 82, 91a, 117b; A KOUPRIANOFF cover (b): ceramic, back cover: tomatoes, 2, 5a, 5b, 6, 7, 8a, 9b, 10b, 12, 13, 15a, 18, 20, 21, 22, 24, 27a, 27b, 32/3, 34, 35, 36, 37b, 39, 40, 41, 43b, 44, 49, 53, 54, 55a, 56, 57, 58, 63a, 64b, 65, 66, 68a, 69, 77a, 78, 79, 84, 85, 81b, 122c; J A TIMS 60; P WILSON 1, 16, 17, 23, 29, 37a, 38, 43a, 45, 46, 50, 55b, 59, 61, 64a, 70, 72, 117a, 122a, 122b

Contributors
Copy editor: Hilary Hughes Page Layout: Design 23 Verifier: Emma Rowley Ruas
Researcher (Practical Matters): Colin Follett Indexer: Marie Lorimer
Revision Management: Apostrophe S Limited

Dear Essential Traveller

Your comments, opinions and recommendations are very important to us. So please help us to improve our travel guides by taking a few minutes to complete this simple questionnaire.

You do not need a stamp (unless posted outside the UK). If you do not want to cut this page from your guide, then photocopy it or write your answers on a plain sheet of paper.

Send to: **The Editor, AA World Travel Guides, FREEPOST SCE 4598, Basingstoke RG21 4GY.**

Your recommendations...

We always encourage readers' recommendations for restaurants, nightlife or shopping – if your recommendation is used in the next edition of the guide, we will send you a *FREE* AA *Essential* **Guide** of your choice. Please state below the establishment name, location and your reasons for recommending it.

_____

_____

_____

_____

Please send me **AA *Essential*** _____

About this guide...

Which title did you buy?

AA *Essential* _____

Where did you buy it? _____

When? m m / y y

Why did you choose an AA *Essential* Guide? _____

_____

_____

_____

_____

Did this guide meet your expectations?

Exceeded ☐ Met all ☐ Met most ☐ Fell below ☐

Please give your reasons _____

_____

_____

_____

continued on next page...

Were there any aspects of this guide that you particularly liked? _____

_____

_____

Is there anything we could have done better? _____

_____

_____

About you...

Name (*Mr/Mrs/Ms*) _____

    Address _____

_____

_____ Postcode _____

    Daytime tel nos _____

Please only give us your mobile phone number if you wish to hear from us about other products and services from the AA and partners by text or mms.

Which age group are you in?

    Under 25 ☐ 25–34 ☐ 35–44 ☐ 45–54 ☐ 55–64 ☐ 65+ ☐

How many trips do you make a year?

    Less than one ☐ One ☐ Two ☐ Three or more ☐

Are you an AA member? Yes ☐ No ☐

About your trip...

When did you book? m m / y y   When did you travel? m m / y y

How long did you stay? _____

Was it for business or leisure? _____

Did you buy any other travel guides for your trip?

    If yes, which ones? _____

Thank you for taking the time to complete this questionnaire. Please send it to us as soon as possible, and remember, you do not need a stamp (*unless posted outside the UK*).

Happy Holidays!